Getting Ready for High-Stakes Assessment

Grade 4

Contents

© Houghton Mifflin Harcourt Publishing Company

About *Getting Ready for High-Stakes Assessment*

This *Getting Ready for High-Stakes Assessment* print guide consists of standards-based practice and practice tests.

Standards-Based Practice

The items in each practice set are designed to give students exposure to the wide variety of ways in which a standard may be assessed.

All standards-based practice sets are available to students online. Online item types include traditional multiple choice as well as technology-enhanced item types that are similar to the ones students will see on actual high-stakes assessments. The online practice experience also offers students hints, corrective feedback, and opportunities to try an item multiple times. You can assign online standards-based practice and receive instant access to student data and reports. The reports can help you pinpoint student strengths and weaknesses and tailor instruction to meet their needs. The standards-based practice sets in this guide mirror those found online; however, some technology-enhanced item types have been modified or replaced with items suitable for paper-and-pencil testing.

Practice Tests

Into Math also includes three practice tests. The practice tests are available online. Online item types include traditional multiple choice as well as technology-enhanced item types that are similar to ones students will see on actual high-stakes assessments. You can assign the online tests for instant access to data and standards alignments. The practice tests in this guide mirror those found online; however, some technology-enhanced item types were modified or replaced with items suitable for paper-and-pencil testing. This guide includes record forms for these tests that show the content focus and depth of knowledge for each item.

Assessment Item Types

High-stakes assessments contain item types beyond the traditional multiple-choice format. This allows for a more robust assessment of students' understanding of concepts and skills. High-stakes assessments are administered via computers, and *Into Math* presents items in formats similar to what students will see on the real tests. The following information is provided to help you familiarize your students with these different types of items. An example of each item type appears on the following pages. You may want to use the examples to introduce the item types to students. These pages describe the most common item types. You may find other types on some tests.

Example 1: Multiselect

Upon first glance, many students may easily confuse this item type with a traditional multiple-choice item. Explain to students that this type of item will have a special direction line that asks them to select all the answers to the problem that are correct.

What equations does this model show?

Select **all** the correct answers.

(A) $4 \times 3 = 12$ (D) $12 = 4 \times 3$

(B) $3 \times 4 = 7$ (E) $4 \times 4 = 16$

(C) $7 = 3 \times 4$

Example 2: Fill in the Blank

Sometimes when students take a digital test, they will have to select a word, number, or symbol from a drop-down list or drag answer options into blanks. The print versions of the *Into Math* tests ask students to write the correct answer in the blank.

Mark's backpack weighs 2,415 g. Lin's backpack weighs 3 kg. How do these masses compare? Write $<$, $>$, or $=$ in the blank.

2,415 g _____ 3 kg

Example 3: Classification

Some *Into Math* assessment items require students to categorize numbers or shapes. Digital versions of this item type require students to drag answer options into the correct place in a table. When the classification involves more complex equations or drawings, each object will have a letter next to it. Print versions of this item type will ask students to write answer options in the correct place in the table. Tell students that sometimes they may write the same number or word in more than one column of the table.

Write the name of each quadrilateral into the correct place in the table. Some quadrilaterals may be used more than once or not at all.

Has 2 Pairs of Parallel Sides	Has 4 Congruent Angles

trapezoid   rectangle

square   rhombus

Example 4: Matching

In some items, students will need to match one set of objects to another. In some computer-based items, students will need to drag an answer option into a box next to the element it matches. On paper-based tests, they do this by drawing a line connecting the two elements that match.

Draw a line to match each expression in the left column with an expression in the right column.

4×6	$7 + 7 + 7 + 7$
4×4	$4 + 4 + 4 + 4$
7×4	$7 + 7$
7×2	$4 + 4 + 4 + 4 + 4 + 4$

Example 5: Choice Matrix

Students may also need to match elements by filling in a table. On the digital tests, they select buttons in the table to indicate the correct answers. On paper-based tests, they place X's in the table to indicate the correct answers.

Place an X in the table to show if each fraction is equivalent to 1.

	Yes	No
$\frac{7}{7}$		
$\frac{7}{1}$		
$\frac{1}{1}$		
$\frac{1}{7}$		

Example 6: Graphing/Number Line

On computerized tests, students will be expected to use a graphing tool to plot points, graph lines, and draw polygons. On paper-based versions of these items, students will plot, graph, or draw on a grid or number line supplied with the item.

Lea's backpack weighs 3 pounds.
José's backpack weighs $3\frac{1}{2}$ pounds.
Cora's backpack weighs more than Lea's backpack but less than José's.

Plot a point on the number line to show the weight of Cora's backpack.

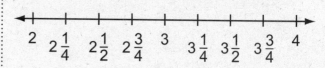

$2 \quad 2\frac{1}{4} \quad 2\frac{1}{2} \quad 2\frac{3}{4} \quad 3 \quad 3\frac{1}{4} \quad 3\frac{1}{2} \quad 3\frac{3}{4} \quad 4$

Example 7: Shading

Shading items allow students to select boxes to shade portions of an interactive rectangular array. In the print versions of these items, students shade a model to show the relationship being assessed.

Shade $\frac{1}{3}$ of the whole model.

Name

1 Which comparison does the model show?

32

| 4 | 4 | 4 | 4 | 4 | 4 | 4 | 4 |

| 4 |

Ⓐ 8 more than 4 is 32.

Ⓑ 9 more than 4 is 32.

Ⓒ 8 times as many as 4 is 32.

Ⓓ 9 times as many as 4 is 32.

2 Nadia buys balloons for a party. She buys 3 times as many purple balloons as yellow balloons. Nadia buys 18 purple balloons.

Which equation tells how many yellow balloons Nadia buys?

Ⓐ $3 \times 6 = 18$

Ⓑ $3 + 15 = 18$

Ⓒ $3 + 18 = 21$

Ⓓ $3 \times 18 = 54$

3 Darlene's dog weighs 5 pounds. Lee's dog weighs 4 times as much as Darlene's. Which equation can be used to find the weight of Lee's dog, n?

Ⓐ $5 \times n = 4$

Ⓑ $5 + n = 4$

Ⓒ $5 + 4 = n$

Ⓓ $5 \times 4 = n$

4 Hal has 3 times as many roses as tulips. He has 15 roses. How many tulips does Hal have?

_____

5 Which equation is represented by the model?

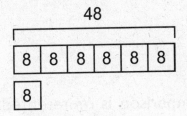

48

| 8 | 8 | 8 | 8 | 8 | 8 |

| 8 |

Ⓐ $6 \times 8 = 48$

Ⓑ $7 \times 8 = 48$

Ⓒ $8 \times 8 = 48$

Ⓓ $8 + 6 = 48$

6 Which number correctly completes the comparison?

6 times as many as _____ is 54.

Ⓐ 8   Ⓒ 48

Ⓑ 9   Ⓓ 60

7 The coach has 9 footballs. She has 3 times as many basketballs. How many basketballs does the coach have?

_____

8 Which comparisons about 42 = 6 × 7 are correct?

Select **all** the correct answers.

Ⓐ 42 is 6 more than 7.
Ⓑ 42 is 7 more than 6.
Ⓒ 6 is 7 times as many as 42.
Ⓓ 7 is 6 times as many as 42.
Ⓔ 42 is 6 times as many as 7.
Ⓕ 42 is 7 times as many as 6.

9 What comparison is represented by the numbers shown in the model?

36

| 9 | 9 | 9 | 9 |

| 9 |

4 times as many as _____ is _____.

10 Which statements are equivalent to the equation 3 × 15 = 45?

Place an X in the table to show if the equation is equivalent to each statement.

	Yes	No
45 is 3 more than 15.		
15 is 5 times as many as 3.		
3 times as many as 15 is 45.		
45 is 15 times as many as 3.		

1 Five students in a class each collected 75 cans for a can drive fundraiser. How many cans did the students bring in for the can drive?

Ⓐ 15   Ⓒ 80

Ⓑ 70   Ⓓ 375

2 Brandon played in 3 basketball games last week. He scored 21 points per game. How many total points did he score last week?

Ⓐ 63 points   Ⓒ 18 points

Ⓑ 24 points   Ⓓ 7 points

3 Li is planning to add baseball cards to his collection. There are 15 cards in each pack of baseball cards. He wants to know how many total cards he will have if he purchases different numbers of packs.

Fill in the blanks with the correct answers from the list.

3 packs = _____ cards

5 packs = _____ cards

7 packs = _____ cards

9 packs = _____ cards

| 105 | 75 | 45 | 135 | 90 |

4 Ava took 18 digital photos on a field trip to the museum. Emily took 3 times as many. How many digital photos did Emily take on the trip?

Ⓐ 6 photos   Ⓑ 15 photos   Ⓒ 54 photos   Ⓓ 64 photos

5 As a goalie for his hockey team, Esteban averages 13 saves a game. He is calculating his total saves for different numbers of games he has played during the season.

Place an X in the table to show if he calculated his total saves correctly or not.

	Calculated Correctly	Calculated Incorrectly
The total number of saves for 2 games is 26 saves.		
The total number of saves for 4 games is 42 saves.		
The total number of saves for 7 games is 81 saves.		
The total number of saves for 10 games is 130 saves.		

6 Mark's family has lived in the same town for 3 years. There are 12 months in a year.

For how many months have they lived in the town?

Ⓐ 24
Ⓑ 32
Ⓒ 36
Ⓓ 60

7 Emily is trying to divide 72 packages of crayons into equal groups for an art project. What would be the total number of packages in each group if she places them into the different groups shown?

Draw a line to match each group with the correct number of packages.

3 groups ●		● 8 packages
6 groups ●		● 9 packages
8 groups ●		● 12 packages
9 groups ●		● 16 packages
		● 24 packages

8 Kate danced for 90 minutes at a dance class. This was 3 times as long as the number of minutes James danced.

For how long did James dance?

Ⓐ 30 minutes
Ⓑ 87 minutes
Ⓒ 93 minutes
Ⓓ 270 minutes

9 Ahmie reads 22 pages of her book each day. At the end of 8 days, how many pages has she read?

Ahmie has read _____ pages.

10 Diego's family is taking a trip to visit his cousins. They will be away for 3 days. There are 24 hours in one day.

For how many hours will they be away?

Ⓐ 24 hours
Ⓑ 36 hours
Ⓒ 48 hours
Ⓓ 72 hours

1 The art teacher needs 30 markers for her morning classes and 40 markers for her afternoon classes. The markers come in packages of 15.

What is the smallest number of packages of markers the art teacher will need to buy?

Ⓐ 5   Ⓒ 3

Ⓑ 4   Ⓓ 2

2 Carrie manages a catering company. She rented 225 chairs each week for the first two weeks of May. Carrie rented 150 chairs each week for the first two weeks of April.

How many chairs did Carrie rent in those four weeks?

Ⓐ 375   Ⓒ 600

Ⓑ 525   Ⓓ 750

3 Lana bought party favors at the store for the school's sixth grade graduation party. Lana bought 7 bags of party hats with 12 hats in each bag. Lana also bought 4 bags of horns with 24 horns in each bag.

How many more horns than party hats did Lana buy?

4 The school principal orders 2 new whiteboards for each grade. There are 3 grades in the school. Each new whiteboard costs $95.

What is the total cost for the new whiteboards?

Ⓐ $196

Ⓑ $475

Ⓒ $570

Ⓓ $855

5 Shari plans to buy either 3 Cinderella rose bushes or 2 America rose bushes. Cinderella rose bushes cost $12 each. America rose bushes cost $19 each. Which rose bushes should Shari buy if she wants to spend the least amount of money?

Ⓐ The Cinderella rose bushes will cost $7 less than the America rose bushes.

Ⓑ The America rose bushes will cost $4 less than the Cinderella rose bushes.

Ⓒ The America rose bushes will cost $2 less than the Cinderella rose bushes.

Ⓓ The Cinderella rose bushes will cost $2 less than the America rose bushes.

Grade 4 • Standards-Based Practice

6 Bill and Alyssa helped pack books for the community center. Bill packed 8 boxes with 30 books in each box. Alyssa packed 9 boxes with 25 books in each box.

How many more books did Bill pack?

7 Nolan has 40 toy cars and 48 toy trucks. He puts his toy cars and trucks into boxes. Each box holds 9 toys.

How many boxes does Nolan need to store all of his toy cars and trucks?

Ⓐ 5

Ⓑ 6

Ⓒ 9

Ⓓ 10

8 In a school auditorium, there are 3 rows that need 2 new seats each. Each new seat costs $74.

What is the cost for the new seats?

9 Kris and Julio played a card game. Together, they scored 36 points in one game. Kris scored two times as many points as Julio.

How many points did Kris score?

10 A kennel is moving 160 dogs to a new building. Each dog has its own crate. The moving truck holds 9 dogs in their crates. The manager plans 17 trips with the truck and wants to know if that will be enough trips to move all the dogs.

Which statement is correct?

Ⓐ This is not enough trips, and there will be 2 crates left over.

Ⓑ This is not enough trips, and there will be 7 crates left over.

Ⓒ This is enough trips, and there is no room left over on the last trip.

Ⓓ This is enough trips, and there will be enough room for 1 more crate on the last trip.

1 Kayla has 36 yellow stickers, 27 red stickers, and 18 blue stickers. She wants to distribute the stickers so that each bag contains only one color of stickers and every bag has the same number of stickers.

How many stickers can Kayla put in each bag?

Ⓐ 1, 2, or 9
Ⓑ 3 or 9
Ⓒ 1, 3, 9, or 18
Ⓓ 1, 3, or 9

2 Select **all** the correct factor pairs of 54.

Ⓐ 1 and 54
Ⓑ 3 and 18
Ⓒ 4 and 50
Ⓓ 6 and 9
Ⓔ 27 and 27

3 Jesse states that 53 is a prime number. Which statement correctly explains why 53 is a prime number?

Ⓐ It is divisible by only 1 and 53.
Ⓑ It has more than two factors.
Ⓒ It is less than 100.
Ⓓ It is an odd number.

4 Each car on a roller coaster has 8 seats. The cars are connected to make a train.

Place an X in the table to show whether each number of seats can be in a roller coaster train.

	Yes	No
32 seats		
42 seats		
48 seats		
54 seats		

5 Josh works in a balloon store. He puts 45 balloons into bunches for a customer. He must use the same number of balloons in each bunch. How many balloons could be in each bunch?

Select **all** the correct answers.

Ⓐ 3
Ⓑ 5
Ⓒ 6
Ⓓ 8
Ⓔ 9

Name _____

6 Douglas is classifying a group of numbers as prime or composite. Which classification is true for each number?

Place an X in the table to show whether each number is prime or composite.

	Prime	Composite
15		
31		
42		
89		
93		

7 Order the factors of 18 and 27 from least to greatest.

Fill in the blanks with the correct numbers from the list.

Factors of 18:

1, ____, ____, ____, ____, 18

Factors of 27:

1, ____, ____, 27

2	3	4	6	9	12	18	27

8 Ellie is performing in a dance recital. Her teacher sets up 7 rows of chairs for the audience. Each row has the same number of chairs.

Which number could be the total number of chairs for the audience?

Ⓐ 20   Ⓒ 32
Ⓑ 25   Ⓓ 35

9 Which numbers are composite?

Select **all** the correct answers.

Ⓐ 17   Ⓓ 57
Ⓑ 28   Ⓔ 61
Ⓒ 45

10 Molly and Brian are playing a game. Molly is counting by 8s. Brian is counting by 6s.

What is the first number they both say?

Ⓐ 12
Ⓑ 16
Ⓒ 24
Ⓓ 32

1 Don creates the following number pattern.

4, 8, 6, 10, 8, 12, 10, 14

What is the next number in his pattern?

Ⓐ 10   Ⓒ 16

Ⓑ 12   Ⓓ 18

2 Ming creates the following number pattern.

24, 21, 23, 20, 22, 19, 21, 18

Her friend, Jack, continues the pattern and writes the next number.

What number should he write?

Ⓐ 15

Ⓑ 16

Ⓒ 20

Ⓓ 21

3 Chen created the following number pattern.

2, 5, 11, 23

What are the next three numbers in this pattern?

2, 5, 11, 23, _____, _____, _____

| 42 | 47 | 81 | 95 | 191 | 212 |

4 Eliza and Diego made a secret code. They wrote some numbers to help them remember the pattern.

8, 11, 10, 13, 12, 15, 14, 17

What should be the next number in the code?

Ⓐ 15

Ⓑ 16

Ⓒ 18

Ⓓ 20

5 Beverley draws a shape pattern.

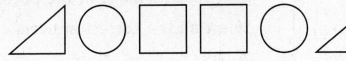

Which shapes does she draw next?

Ⓐ triangle, circle

Ⓑ circle, square

Ⓒ square, square

Ⓓ square, circle

6 Amelia is completing the following pattern.

3, 6, _____, 12, 15

What number is missing from the middle of the pattern?

_____

7 Inez draws the first five shapes following a pattern.

What are the next two shapes that she draws?

Ⓐ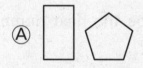

Ⓑ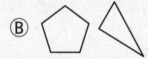

Ⓒ

Ⓓ

8 Jose created a number pattern. He starts his pattern by writing the number 36. If his rule is "Add 6," what is the fourth number in Jose's pattern?

_____

9 Jason creates a pattern based on adding 1 and multiplying by 2. His pattern starts with the number 1.

Place an X in the table to show if each number is one of the next three numbers in the pattern.

	Part of the Pattern	Not Part of the Pattern
3		
4		
7		
10		
22		

10 Brianna created a pattern using this rule: Add 8, subtract 4.

She begins the pattern with the number 9, followed by 13.

Which of these will be one of the next four numbers in the pattern?

Select **all** the correct answers.

Ⓐ 17

Ⓑ 19

Ⓒ 21

Ⓓ 23

Ⓔ 25

1 How many times the value of the 9 in 92,175 is the value of the 9 in 924,512?

(A) 100   (C) 10

(B) 90   (D) 9

2 What is the value of the 2 in 724,638?

(A) 200   (C) 20,000

(B) 2,000   (D) 200,000

3 Place an X in the table to show the value of the 5 in each number.

	5	50	5,000	50,000
18,005				
36,458				
52,789				
375,123				

4 Carson made a four-digit number with a 4 in the thousands place, a 4 in the ones place, a 5 in the tens place, and a 6 in the hundreds place. What was the number?

(A) 4,456   (C) 4,564

(B) 4,465   (D) 4,654

5 Place an X in the table to show if each statement is true or false.

	True	False
The value of 9 in 874,092 is 900.		
The value of 2 in 724,638 is 20,000.		
The value of 8 in 380,194 is 800,000.		
The value of 7 in 671,235 is 70,000.		

© Houghton Mifflin Harcourt Publishing Company

6 Kevin got 738,256 hits on his new website. What is the value of the digit 7 in 738,256?

Ⓐ 7,000 Ⓒ 700,000

Ⓑ 70,000 Ⓓ 7,000,000

7 What is the value of the 8 in 380,194?

Ⓐ 80 Ⓒ 8,000

Ⓑ 800 Ⓓ 80,000

8 Saskia scored 157,834 points on the third level of her computer game. What is the value of the digit 5 in 157,834?

_____

9 How many times the value of the 4 in 4,175 is the value of the 4 in 43,512?

Ⓐ 4 Ⓒ 100

Ⓑ 40 Ⓓ 10

10 A large puzzle contains 172,435 pieces. What is the value of the digit 2 in 172,435?

Ⓐ 200 Ⓒ 20,000

Ⓑ 2,000 Ⓓ 200,000

11 How many times the value of the 5 in 51,327 is the value of the 5 in 502,428?

Ⓐ 1 Ⓒ 50

Ⓑ 10 Ⓓ 100

12 How many times the value of the 7 in 72 is the value of the 7 in 7,429?

Ⓐ 1 Ⓒ 70

Ⓑ 10 Ⓓ 100

13 Fill in the blank with a number from the list to correctly complete the sentence.

The value of the 2 in 201 is _____ times the value of the 2 in 27.

1	10	100	200

14 Fill in the blank with a number from the list to correctly complete the sentence.

The value of the 8 in 8,491 is _____ times the value of the 8 in 843.

10	800	1,000	8,000

1 The heights of three mountain peaks in Colorado are listed.

Blanca Peak: 14,345 feet

Crestone Peak: 14,294 feet

Humboldt Peak: 14,064 feet

Place an X in the table to show if each mountain peak height in feet is between 14,000 and 14,300 or between 14,301 and 14,500.

	Between 14,000 Feet and 14,300 Feet	Between 14,301 Feet and 14,500 Feet
Blanca Peak		
Crestone Peak		
Humboldt Peak		

2 A state governor compares the populations of five cities in her state.

City	Population
Easton	286,152
Springfield	301,673
Fairview	322,694
Greenville	249,866
Madison	320,145

Fill in the blanks with the correct symbols (< , >) to compare the populations.

Easton population _____ Greenville population

Springfield population _____ Madison population

3 Select **all** the answers that show 403,871.

Ⓐ four hundred three thousand, eight hundred one

Ⓑ four hundred three thousand, seventy-one

Ⓒ four hundred three thousand, eight hundred seventy-one

Ⓓ 400,000 + 38,000 + 800 + 70 + 1

Ⓔ 400,000 + 3,000 + 800 + 70 + 1

Ⓕ 4 hundred thousands + 3 thousands + 8 hundreds + 7 tens + 1 one

Name _____

4 Select **all** the numbers that will make a correct comparison.

807,058 > ☐

Ⓐ 870,508

Ⓑ 870,058

Ⓒ 807,508

Ⓓ 807,085

Ⓔ 805,058

Ⓕ 800,758

5 Maya used number tiles to make the number 428,745. Then she changed two digits to make the number 427,845.

Which statement about these numbers is correct?

Ⓐ 428,745 < 427,845

Ⓑ 427,845 = 428,745

Ⓒ 427,845 > 428,745

Ⓓ 427,845 < 428,745

6 The heights of mountain peaks in Canada are listed.

Name	Height (in feet)
Centennial Peak	12,533
Mount Columbia	12,293
Mount King George	12,274
Mount Root	12,799

Which is the tallest peak?

Ⓐ Centennial Peak

Ⓑ Mount Columbia

Ⓒ Mount King George

Ⓓ Mount Root

7 Place an X in the table to show the value of the 5 in each number.

	5	50	5,000	50,000
36,458				
375,123				
18,005				
52,789				

8 A college basketball team had three games in April. Game one had an attendance of 14,753 people. Game two had an attendance of 20,320 people. Game three had an attendance of 14,505 people.

Write the game numbers in the boxes in order from LEAST attendance to GREATEST attendance.

LEAST   GREATEST

☐   ☐   ☐

14

1 There were 12,351 visitors to a history center in the past year. What is the number of visitors when rounded to the nearest hundred?

Ⓐ 12,300

Ⓑ 12,350

Ⓒ 12,360

Ⓓ 12,400

2 Stephanie is rounding numbers to the nearest ten. What is the rounded value for each of the numbers?

Write the correct rounded number from the list in the table next to each of the original numbers.

You will not use all the numbers.

Original Number	Rounded Number
636	
645	
982	
987	

600	640	650	900	980	990

3 Diego counted the total weekend ticket sales for the school musical. There were 1,918 tickets sold. Diego rounded the number to the nearest thousand for a school article he wrote about the musical.

What number did he include in the article?

Ⓐ 1,000

Ⓑ 1,900

Ⓒ 1,920

Ⓓ 2,000

4 Frankie rounded 18,762 to the nearest thousand. What number did he round to?

_____

5 What is 25,264 rounded to the nearest hundred?

Ⓐ 25,000

Ⓑ 25,260

Ⓒ 25,300

Ⓓ 30,000

6 The total season attendance for a professional football team's home games, rounded to the nearest ten thousand, was 710,000.

Place an X in the table to show whether or not each number could be the exact attendance.

	Yes	No
700,987		
701,752		
706,791		
714,498		

7 What is 5,418 rounded to the nearest ten?

Ⓐ 5,400

Ⓑ 5,410

Ⓒ 5,420

Ⓓ 5,500

8 The total season attendance for a college team's home games was 270,000 when rounded to the nearest ten thousand.

Which number might be the exact attendance?

Ⓐ 206,636

Ⓑ 260,987

Ⓒ 265,888

Ⓓ 276,499

9 Georgia rounds four numbers to the nearest hundred. What is the rounded value for each number?

Write the correct rounded number from the list in the table next to each of the original numbers.

Numbers may be used more than once or not at all.

Original Number	Rounded Number
2,098	
2,136	
2,175	
2,245	

| 2,000   2,100   2,200   2,300 |

10 Tyrone rounded a number to the nearest hundred, resulting in 2,600. What number might he have rounded to the nearest hundred?

Select **all** the correct answers.

Ⓐ 2,498

Ⓑ 2,513

Ⓒ 2,576

Ⓓ 2,639

Ⓔ 2,681

1 What is the sum of 65,182 and 58,458?

(A) 113,640

(B) 123,540

(C) 123,630

(D) 123,640

2 What is the sum?

101,452 + 72,863 + 5,391

_____

3 What is the difference between 73,815 and 48,968?

(A) 24,847

(B) 24,947

(C) 25,847

(D) 34,847

4 What is the difference?

547,262 − 256,089

_____

5 What is the sum of 35,698 and 48,735?

(A) 84,433

(B) 84,423

(C) 84,333

(D) 74,433

6 What is the difference?

82,458 − 56,759

(A) 35,699

(B) 25,789

(C) 25,699

(D) 25,409

7 What is the answer for each of the problems?

Fill in the blanks with the correct answers from the list to complete the sentences.

The sum of 444,276 and 32,987 is _____.

The difference of 496,784 and 7,893 is _____.

477,363	477,263	478,263
487,891	488,891	

Name _____

8 A subtraction problem is shown with one number unknown.

$$256{,}102$$
$$-\ 1\ \square\ 7{,}768$$
$$\overline{128{,}334}$$

Which number completes the problem?

Ⓐ 1

Ⓑ 2

Ⓒ 3

Ⓓ 4

---

9 What is the sum of the addition problem shown?

$$279{,}987$$
$$45{,}201$$
$$+\quad 7{,}470$$

---

10 An addition problem is shown with one number missing.

$$726{,}392$$
$$+\ 1\ \square\ {,}872$$
$$\overline{744{,}264}$$

Which of these is the unknown number?

Ⓐ 2

Ⓑ 4

Ⓒ 7

Ⓓ 8

1 What is the product of 3,650 × 6?

Ⓐ 612

Ⓑ 3,646

Ⓒ 3,656

Ⓓ 21,900

2 What is the value of this product?

325 × $7

Ⓐ $2,125

Ⓑ $2,145

Ⓒ $2,175

Ⓓ $2,275

3 What is the product of 20 × 12?

Ⓐ 120   Ⓒ 240

Ⓑ 200   Ⓓ 360

4 What is the value of each product?

Fill in the blanks with the correct numbers from the list.

14 × 30 = _____

20 × 14 = _____

30 × 60 = _____

50 × 50 = _____

240	280	420
1,800	2,100	2,500

5 Which equations were multiplied correctly and which were multiplied incorrectly?

Place an X in the table to show whether the equations are correct or incorrect.

	Correct	Incorrect
4 × 938 = 3,652		
6 × 723 = 4,228		
7 × 3,249 = 22,743		
9 × 2,641 = 23,769		

6 What is the product of 15 × 24?

Ⓐ 180

Ⓑ 300

Ⓒ 360

Ⓓ 380

7 What is the product of 28 × 12?

Ⓐ 280

Ⓑ 308

Ⓒ 336

Ⓓ 364

8 What is the solution to the equation 1,251 × 5 = ▢?

_____

9 What is the product of 22 × 43?

Ⓐ 726

Ⓑ 946

Ⓒ 990

Ⓓ 1,166

10 What is the product of 4 × 1,832?

_____

11 What is the product of 2,486 × 3?

Ⓐ 6,448

Ⓑ 6,458

Ⓒ 7,448

Ⓓ 7,458

1 What is the quotient of 749 ÷ 7?

Ⓐ 17   Ⓒ 117

Ⓑ 107   Ⓓ 170

2 Which of the division problems has a quotient equal to 600?

Place an X in the table to show the correct response to each equation.

	Equal to 600	Not Equal to 600
1,200 ÷ 2 =		
2,400 ÷ 6 =		
420 ÷ 7 =		
3,000 ÷ 5 =		

3 Which quotient has a value of 120?

Ⓐ 500 ÷ 5

Ⓑ 600 ÷ 5

Ⓒ 700 ÷ 5

Ⓓ 800 ÷ 5

4 What is the value of this quotient?

228 ÷ 4

Ⓐ 57   Ⓒ 517

Ⓑ 507   Ⓓ 570

5 What is the value of this quotient?

925 ÷ 5

Name _____

6 Draw a line from each quotient to its value. You may use some values more than once or not at all.

$360 \div 3$	●	●	
$360 \div 4$	●	●	
$480 \div 3$	●	●	
$480 \div 4$	●	●	
		●	

7 What is the answer to this division problem?

$543 \div 7 = \square$

Ⓐ 77

Ⓑ 77 r4

Ⓒ 77 r6

Ⓓ 78

8 Which quotients are equal to 200?

Select **all** the correct answers.

Ⓐ $400 \div 2 = \square$

Ⓑ $600 \div 3 = \square$

Ⓒ $800 \div 8 = \square$

Ⓓ $1,000 \div 5 = \square$

Ⓔ $1,600 \div 4 = \square$

9 What is the remainder for each of these quotients?
Fill in the blanks with the correct numbers from the list.

$1,204 \div 6 = 200 \text{ r}\_\_\_\_\_$

$363 \div 9 = 40 \text{ r}\_\_\_\_\_$

$428 \div 7 = 61 \text{ r}\_\_\_\_\_$

$905 \div 3 = 301 \text{ r}\_\_\_\_\_$

0	1	2	3	4

10 What is the value of this quotient?

$118 \div 6$

Ⓐ 19

Ⓑ 19 r2

Ⓒ 19 r4

Ⓓ 20

1 Andy walked $\frac{3}{4}$ of a mile to the post office and another $\frac{1}{2}$ mile to the supermarket. Which number is a common denominator for $\frac{3}{4}$ and $\frac{1}{2}$?

Ⓐ 10   Ⓒ 6

Ⓑ 8   Ⓓ 5

2 Simon bought $\frac{6}{8}$ of a pound of tuna salad for sandwiches. Which fraction is equivalent to $\frac{6}{8}$?

Ⓐ $\frac{2}{4}$ Ⓒ $\frac{2}{3}$

Ⓑ $\frac{1}{2}$ Ⓓ $\frac{12}{16}$

3 Collin drew two fraction models.

Did Collin draw models of equivalent fractions?

Ⓐ Yes, because the models are the same size.

Ⓑ Yes, because the same size part of each model is shaded.

Ⓒ No, because the shaded parts in each model are different sizes.

Ⓓ No, because the models have different numbers of shaded parts.

4 Fill in the blanks with the correct symbols (=, ≠) to show if the fractions are equivalent or not equivalent.

$\frac{3}{4}$ _____ $\frac{6}{8}$

$\frac{2}{3}$ _____ $\frac{8}{12}$

$\frac{3}{6}$ _____ $\frac{2}{3}$

$\frac{4}{10}$ _____ $\frac{2}{5}$

5 Fill in the boxes with the correct numbers from the list to generate equivalent fractions for $\frac{1}{2}$. You will not use all the numbers.

$$\frac{1}{2} = \frac{\Box}{6} = \frac{4}{\Box} = \frac{\Box}{\Box}$$

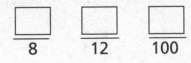

| 2 | 3 | 5 | 6 | 8 | 9 | 12 |

6 Nicolette needs $\frac{1}{4}$ yard of fabric for her quilt. Write $\frac{1}{4}$ as an equivalent fraction with the denominators shown.

Fill in the boxes with the correct answers.

$\dfrac{\Box}{8}$ $\dfrac{\Box}{12}$ $\dfrac{\Box}{100}$

7 In Jason's homeroom, $\frac{3}{6}$ of the students like soccer best, $\frac{4}{12}$ of the students like volleyball best, and $\frac{2}{12}$ of the students like baseball best.

Place an X in the table to show if each statement is true or false.

	True	False
In simplest form, $\frac{1}{3}$ of the students like soccer best.		
In simplest form, $\frac{1}{4}$ of the students like volleyball best.		
In simplest form, $\frac{1}{6}$ of the students like baseball best.		

8 Kayla draws a model to show the fraction $\frac{8}{12}$. Then she draws another model to show the fraction $\frac{4}{6}$. Both models have the same length.

Select **all** the correct statements about the two models.

Ⓐ The same amount of each model is shaded.

Ⓑ The models have the same number of parts.

Ⓒ The model for $\frac{8}{12}$ has four more parts than the model for $\frac{4}{6}$.

Ⓓ The model for $\frac{8}{12}$ has more shaded parts than the model for $\frac{4}{6}$.

Ⓔ The parts in the model for $\frac{8}{12}$ are twice the size of the parts in the model for $\frac{4}{6}$.

9 Natalie draws a model of fraction A. Then she divides each part of the model into equal sections to model fraction B, which is equivalent to fraction A. The model for fraction B has 8 shaded sections.

Which of these could be fraction A?

Ⓐ $\frac{3}{4}$ Ⓑ $\frac{4}{5}$ Ⓒ $\frac{8}{12}$ Ⓓ $\frac{5}{10}$

1 Jasmine cut $\frac{3}{8}$ yard of blue ribbon and $\frac{1}{3}$ yard of red ribbon to decorate a package. Which statement correctly compares the fractions?

Ⓐ $\frac{1}{3} > \frac{3}{8}$　　　　Ⓒ $\frac{3}{8} > \frac{1}{3}$

Ⓑ $\frac{1}{3} = \frac{3}{8}$　　　　Ⓓ $\frac{3}{8} < \frac{1}{3}$

2 Juan's mother gave him a recipe for trail mix with the ingredients and measurements listed.

Fill in the boxes with the ingredients so that the fractions are correctly ordered from LEAST on the top to the GREATEST on the bottom.

$\frac{3}{4}$ cup cereal

$\frac{1}{4}$ cup peanuts

$\frac{2}{3}$ cup almonds

$\frac{1}{2}$ cup raisins

3 Nori bought $\frac{2}{3}$ pound of chicken salad and $\frac{3}{4}$ pound of tuna salad for a picnic. Which statement correctly compares the fractions?

Ⓐ $\frac{2}{3} > \frac{3}{4}$

Ⓑ $\frac{3}{4} > \frac{2}{3}$

Ⓒ $\frac{2}{3} = \frac{3}{4}$

Ⓓ $\frac{3}{4} < \frac{2}{3}$

4 Darcy bought $\frac{1}{2}$ pound of cheese and $\frac{3}{4}$ pound of hamburger for a barbecue. Compare the amounts of cheese and hamburger that Darcy bought.

Fill in the boxes with the correct answers from the list to compare the fractions.

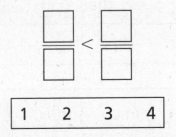

1	2	3	4

Name _____

5 Anita mixes $\frac{3}{5}$ pound of peanuts with $\frac{3}{8}$ pound of raisins to make a snack. Which statement correctly compares the fractions?

Ⓐ $\frac{3}{8} = \frac{3}{5}$

Ⓑ $\frac{3}{8} > \frac{3}{5}$

Ⓒ $\frac{3}{5} > \frac{3}{8}$

Ⓓ $\frac{3}{5} < \frac{3}{8}$

6 Which statements are true?

Select **all** true statements.

Ⓐ $\frac{60}{100} < \frac{4}{5}$

Ⓑ $\frac{4}{5} < \frac{30}{100}$

Ⓒ $\frac{4}{10} < \frac{3}{5} < \frac{70}{100}$

Ⓓ $\frac{1}{4} = \frac{2}{8} = \frac{3}{12}$

Ⓔ $\frac{2}{3} = \frac{4}{6} < \frac{1}{3}$

7 Nicolette needs $\frac{1}{2}$ yard of fabric for her quilt. Write $\frac{1}{2}$ as an equivalent fraction with the denominators shown.

Fill in the boxes with the correct answers from the list to write equivalent fractions.

$$\frac{\boxed{}}{6} = \frac{\boxed{}}{8} = \frac{\boxed{}}{10} = \frac{\boxed{}}{12}$$

2	3	4	5	6	8

8 What is the unknown value to make the statement true?

$$\frac{\boxed{}}{8} > \frac{2}{3}$$

Ⓐ 3   Ⓒ 5

Ⓑ 4   Ⓓ 6

9 Juan has wrenches with the sizes listed.

Fill in the table with the correct answers from the list to order the wrench sizes from LEAST to GREATEST.

Less than $\frac{1}{2}$ in.	Equal to $\frac{1}{2}$ in.	Greater than $\frac{1}{2}$ in.

$\frac{4}{8}$ in.	$\frac{3}{4}$ in.	$\frac{5}{12}$ in.

1 What is $\frac{3}{6} + \frac{2}{6}$?

Ⓐ $\frac{1}{6}$ Ⓒ $\frac{5}{6}$

Ⓑ $\frac{5}{12}$ Ⓓ $\frac{6}{6}$

2 Which equations are true?

Place an X in the table to show whether each equation is true or false.

	True	False
$\frac{1}{4} + \frac{2}{4} = \frac{3}{8}$		
$\frac{2}{8} + \frac{5}{8} = \frac{7}{8}$		
$\frac{7}{10} - \frac{2}{10} = \frac{5}{10}$		
$\frac{5}{12} + \frac{3}{12} = \frac{2}{12}$		

3 Matthew draws a model to help him solve a problem. He divides a bar into 8 equal parts and shades 5 parts. Then he crosses out 2 of the shaded parts.

Which equation does Matthew's model show?

Ⓐ $\frac{5}{8} - \frac{2}{8} = \frac{3}{8}$

Ⓑ $\frac{5}{8} - \frac{2}{5} = \frac{3}{3}$

Ⓒ $\frac{5}{8} + \frac{2}{8} = \frac{7}{8}$

Ⓓ $\frac{8}{5} - \frac{2}{5} = \frac{6}{5}$

4 Cindy has two jars of paint. One jar is $\frac{3}{8}$ full. The other jar is $\frac{2}{8}$ full. What fraction of a jar of paint does Cindy have?

Fill in the blanks with the correct answers from the list to represent and solve the problem.

$\frac{3}{8}$ _____ _____ = _____

| $\frac{1}{8}$ | $\frac{2}{8}$ | $\frac{5}{8}$ | $\frac{7}{8}$ | − | + |

5 On Monday morning, Erin measures $\frac{3}{4}$ inch of snowfall. It continues to snow throughout the day. At the end of the day, there are $\frac{5}{4}$ inches of snow. How many more inches of snow fell?

Ⓐ $\frac{2}{8}$ Ⓒ $\frac{8}{8}$

Ⓑ $\frac{2}{4}$ Ⓓ $\frac{8}{4}$

6 Betsy brought $\frac{6}{12}$ pound of trail mix on a camping trip. She ate $\frac{4}{12}$ pound of the trail mix. How many pounds of trail mix does she have left?

Ⓐ $\frac{2}{12}$ Ⓒ $\frac{2}{6}$

Ⓑ $\frac{2}{10}$ Ⓓ $\frac{10}{12}$

© Houghton Mifflin Harcourt Publishing Company

7 Andrew takes piano lessons. Each day he writes down the number of hours he practices. This is the equation Andrew uses to calculate the number of hours he practiced this week.

$$1\frac{1}{4} + 2 + 1\frac{2}{4} + 1\frac{2}{4} + 1\frac{1}{4} = 6\frac{6}{16}$$

What error did Andrew make in his equation?

Ⓐ Andrew added the numerators incorrectly.

Ⓑ Andrew did not include the 2 hours in the sum.

Ⓒ Andrew added the denominators and the numerators.

Ⓓ Andrew added the denominators instead of the numerators.

8 Mindi planted beans in $\frac{4}{10}$ of her garden and peas in $\frac{5}{10}$ of her garden. What fraction of the garden has beans, and what fraction of the garden is planted with beans or peas?

Plot and label the points on the correct locations on the number line.

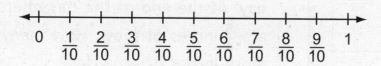

9 Carmen adds two fractions with the same denominator. The sum is less than one whole.

Which fractions could Carmen have added?

Ⓐ $\frac{3}{5} + \frac{4}{5}$

Ⓑ $\frac{2}{6} + \frac{5}{6}$

Ⓒ $\frac{5}{8} + \frac{3}{8}$

Ⓓ $\frac{3}{10} + \frac{2}{10}$

10 On Saturday morning, Jesse played basketball for $\frac{2}{3}$ hour. Later in the day, he played basketball again. He played $2\frac{1}{3}$ hours in all.

How long did Jesse play basketball later in the day?

_____

1 Lamar's mom sells sports equipment online. She sold $\frac{9}{10}$ of the sports equipment she had in stock. What are the different ways $\frac{9}{10}$ can be written as a sum of fractions?

Select the **three** correct answers.

Ⓐ $\frac{3}{10} + \frac{2}{10} + \frac{3}{10} + \frac{1}{10}$

Ⓑ $\frac{2}{10} + \frac{2}{10} + \frac{2}{10} + \frac{2}{10}$

Ⓒ $\frac{2}{10} + \frac{2}{10} + \frac{2}{10} + \frac{3}{10}$

Ⓓ $\frac{4}{10} + \frac{1}{10} + \frac{1}{10} + \frac{3}{10}$

Ⓔ $\frac{4}{10} + \frac{3}{10} + \frac{1}{10} + \frac{1}{10} + \frac{1}{10}$

2 Which statements are equal to $\frac{7}{8}$?

Place an X in the table to show if the statement is equal or not.

	Equal to $\frac{7}{8}$	Not Equal to $\frac{7}{8}$
$\frac{5}{8} + \frac{1}{8} + \frac{1}{8}$		
$\frac{1}{8} + \frac{4}{8} + \frac{1}{8}$		
$\frac{1}{8} + \frac{2}{8} + \frac{2}{8} + \frac{2}{8}$		
$\frac{1}{8} + \frac{1}{8} + \frac{1}{8} + \frac{1}{8} + \frac{2}{8}$		

3 Dillon sells golf balls at a yard sale. He sells $\frac{4}{5}$ of the golf balls. Which of these are ways $\frac{4}{5}$ can be written as a sum of fractions?

Select the **three** correct answers.

Ⓐ $\frac{1}{5} + \frac{1}{5} + \frac{2}{5}$

Ⓑ $\frac{1}{5} + \frac{1}{5} + \frac{1}{5}$

Ⓒ $\frac{1}{5} + \frac{2}{5} + \frac{1}{5}$

Ⓓ $\frac{1}{5} + \frac{1}{5} + \frac{1}{5} + \frac{1}{5}$

Ⓔ $\frac{1}{5} + \frac{1}{5} + \frac{1}{5} + \frac{1}{5} + \frac{1}{5}$

4 Jerry is writing a fraction expression that is equivalent to $\frac{4}{12} + \frac{6}{12} + \frac{1}{12}$.

What is the unknown number that makes the two expressions equal?

$\frac{\square}{12} + \frac{1}{12} + \frac{2}{12} + \frac{3}{12}$

5 Two equations are shown. Each equation is missing the same numerator.

$\frac{1}{6} + \frac{\square}{6} + \frac{1}{6} + \frac{1}{6} = \frac{5}{6}$

$\frac{2}{6} + \frac{1}{6} + \frac{\square}{6} = \frac{5}{6}$

What is the unknown number in the equations?

Ⓐ 1

Ⓑ 2

Ⓒ 3

Ⓓ 4

Name _____

6 Each model is shaded to represent a different fraction.

Image 1

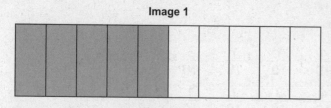

Image 2

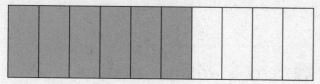

Which expressions have the same value as one of the models?

Write each expression in the correct box to show which image it is equal to.

Image 1

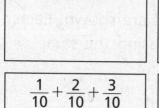

Image 2

$\frac{1}{10} + \frac{2}{10} + \frac{3}{10}$ $\frac{1}{10} + \frac{1}{10} + \frac{3}{10} + \frac{1}{10}$

$\frac{1}{10} + \frac{1}{10} + \frac{1}{10} + \frac{2}{10}$ $\frac{1}{10} + \frac{1}{10} + \frac{2}{10} + \frac{1}{10}$

7 Which expression has the same value as $\frac{8}{100} + \frac{8}{100} + \frac{2}{100} + \frac{6}{100}$?

Ⓐ $\frac{15}{100} + \frac{6}{100} + \frac{1}{100}$

Ⓑ $\frac{5}{100} + \frac{17}{100} + \frac{3}{100}$

Ⓒ $\frac{11}{100} + \frac{10}{100} + \frac{1}{100} + \frac{1}{100}$

Ⓓ $\frac{7}{100} + \frac{9}{100} + \frac{4}{100} + \frac{4}{100}$

8 Kai modeled a fraction by shading parts of the circle as shown.

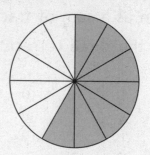

How can the fraction be written as a sum of fractions?

Select the **three** correct answers.

Ⓐ $\frac{2}{12} + \frac{4}{12} + \frac{1}{12}$

Ⓑ $\frac{5}{12} + \frac{1}{12} + \frac{1}{12} + \frac{1}{12}$

Ⓒ $\frac{1}{12} + \frac{4}{12} + \frac{1}{12} + \frac{1}{12}$

Ⓓ $\frac{3}{12} + \frac{1}{12} + \frac{1}{12} + \frac{1}{12} + \frac{2}{12}$

Ⓔ $\frac{1}{12} + \frac{1}{12} + \frac{1}{12} + \frac{1}{12} + \frac{1}{12} + \frac{2}{12}$

9 What fraction makes each equation equal to $\frac{11}{4}$?

Fill in the boxes with the correct fractions from the list to complete the equation. Answers may be used more than once or not at all.

$\frac{5}{4} + \boxed{} + \frac{1}{4} + \frac{3}{4} = \frac{11}{4}$

$\frac{4}{4} + \frac{1}{4} + \boxed{} + \frac{3}{4} + \frac{1}{4} = \frac{11}{4}$

$\frac{1}{4} + \frac{1}{4} + \frac{3}{4} + \boxed{} + \frac{2}{4} = \frac{11}{4}$

| $\frac{1}{4}$ | $\frac{2}{4}$ | $\frac{3}{4}$ | $\frac{4}{4}$ |

1 Zoey has $8\frac{1}{3}$ feet of blue yarn and $4\frac{2}{3}$ feet of green yarn.

How much more blue yarn does Zoey have than green yarn?

Ⓐ $3\frac{1}{3}$ feet   Ⓒ $4\frac{1}{3}$ feet

Ⓑ $3\frac{2}{3}$ feet   Ⓓ $4\frac{2}{3}$ feet

---

2 To get the correct color, Johan mixed $3\frac{1}{4}$ quarts of white paint, $1\frac{3}{4}$ quarts of blue paint, and $2\frac{3}{4}$ quarts of green paint.

How many quarts of paint did Johan mix?

---

3 Which of these addition statements is true?

Place an X in the table to show whether each statement is true or false.

	True	False
$6\frac{7}{10} + 2\frac{1}{10}$ is equal to $4\frac{8}{10}$		
$1\frac{2}{8} + 3\frac{7}{8}$ is equal to $4\frac{1}{8}$		
$1\frac{3}{5} + 2\frac{4}{5}$ is equal to $4\frac{2}{5}$		

---

4 What are the solutions to each of these equations?

Draw a line from the mixed number to the number sentence it matches.

$4\frac{3}{5} + 2\frac{4}{5} = \boxed{}$ •

$9\frac{3}{5} - 2\frac{4}{5} = \boxed{}$ •

• $\boxed{7\frac{2}{5}}$

• $\boxed{7\frac{4}{5}}$

• $\boxed{6\frac{2}{5}}$

• $\boxed{6\frac{4}{5}}$

5 Emma has $5\frac{3}{8}$ pounds of potato salad and $2\frac{7}{8}$ pounds of egg salad for a picnic.

How many more pounds of potato salad than egg salad does Emma have?

Ⓐ 3 pounds

Ⓑ $2\frac{6}{8}$ pounds

Ⓒ $2\frac{4}{8}$ pounds

Ⓓ $2\frac{2}{8}$ pounds

6 An addition problem is shown.

$$2\frac{2}{8} + 3\frac{\boxed{}}{8} = 6\frac{1}{8}$$

What is the unknown digit?

Ⓐ 1

Ⓑ 3

Ⓒ 5

Ⓓ 7

7 SuLee has $3\frac{3}{4}$ yards of purple fabric and $4\frac{2}{4}$ yards of gold fabric.

How many yards of fabric does SuLee have in all?

8 What is the difference of $6\frac{4}{12}$ and $3\frac{5}{12}$?

Ⓐ $2\frac{11}{12}$

Ⓑ $3\frac{1}{12}$

Ⓒ $3\frac{10}{12}$

Ⓓ $3\frac{11}{12}$

9 Sarah has $6\frac{2}{4}$ meters of rope and $3\frac{3}{4}$ meters of string.

How much more rope does Sarah have than string?

Ⓐ $2\frac{1}{4}$ meters

Ⓑ $2\frac{2}{4}$ meters

Ⓒ $2\frac{3}{4}$ meters

Ⓓ $2\frac{4}{4}$ meters

10 What is the sum of $7\frac{4}{6}$ and $3\frac{5}{6}$?

Ⓐ $10\frac{1}{6}$

Ⓑ $10\frac{3}{6}$

Ⓒ $11\frac{1}{6}$

Ⓓ $11\frac{3}{6}$

1 Irene bought $\frac{3}{8}$ pound of wheat flour and $\frac{4}{8}$ pound of rye flour to use in a bread recipe. How many pounds of flour did Irene buy in all?

Ⓐ $\frac{1}{8}$ Ⓑ $\frac{7}{16}$ Ⓒ $\frac{6}{8}$ Ⓓ $\frac{7}{8}$

2 Ben uses $\frac{3}{12}$ pound of strawberries and $\frac{2}{12}$ pound of blueberries to make jam. How many pounds of berries does Ben use to make jam?

Shade the model to show the amount of berries Ben uses to make jam. The model represents 1 pound.

3 Dan has a piece of wood that is $\frac{9}{10}$ meter long. He uses $\frac{6}{10}$ meter of the piece of wood for a model boat he is building. How much of the piece of wood does Dan have left?

Ⓐ $\frac{15}{10}$ meters   Ⓒ $\frac{5}{10}$ meter

Ⓑ $\frac{6}{10}$ meter   Ⓓ $\frac{3}{10}$ meter

4 Ellen needs $\frac{5}{8}$ yard of fringe for her scarf. Ling needs $\frac{2}{8}$ yard of fringe for her scarf. How many more yards of fringe does Ellen need than Ling?

_____

5 Tally's baby sister eats $\frac{1}{4}$ cup of rice cereal on Monday and $\frac{1}{4}$ cup on Tuesday. The baby eats $\frac{2}{4}$ cup of rice cereal on Wednesday. How much rice cereal does the baby eat in all?

Ⓐ $\frac{6}{4}$ cup   Ⓒ $\frac{4}{4}$ cup

Ⓑ $\frac{1}{4}$ cup   Ⓓ $\frac{3}{4}$ cup

6 Jack has two jars of wax. One jar is $\frac{1}{6}$ full. The other jar is $\frac{4}{6}$ full. What equation can be used to show the total amount of wax?

Fill in the boxes with the correct fractions from the list to complete the equation. You will not use all the fractions.

☐ + ☐ = ☐

| $\frac{1}{6}$ | $\frac{2}{6}$ | $\frac{3}{6}$ | $\frac{4}{6}$ | $\frac{5}{6}$ |

Name _____

7 The school carnival is divided into sections. The dunk tanks are in $\frac{1}{10}$ of the carnival. Games are in $\frac{4}{10}$ of the carnival. Student exhibits are in $\frac{5}{10}$ of the carnival.

Which statements are true about the space used for each section of the carnival?

Select **all** the correct statements.

Ⓐ The part of the carnival with games and student exhibits is $\frac{9}{10}$.

Ⓑ The part of the carnival with dunk tanks and student exhibits is $\frac{6}{20}$.

Ⓒ The part of the carnival with games is $\frac{3}{10}$ greater than the part with dunk tanks.

Ⓓ The part of the carnival with student exhibits is $\frac{9}{10}$ greater than the part with games.

Ⓔ The part of the carnival with student exhibits is equal to the part of the carnival with dunk tanks and games.

---

8 Rebecca and Nora used pan balances to weigh bags of sand. Rebecca's bag weighed $\frac{6}{10}$ pound. Nora's bag weighed $\frac{2}{10}$ pound less than Rebecca's bag. How much did Nora's bag of sand weigh?

Plot and label points on the number line to show the number of pounds each person's bag of sand weighs.

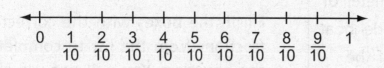

---

9 Harrison ate $\frac{3}{12}$ of a sushi roll. Miles ate $\frac{4}{12}$ of the same sushi roll. How much more of the sushi roll did Miles eat than Harrison?

Ⓐ $\frac{1}{12}$ Ⓑ $\frac{1}{6}$ Ⓒ $\frac{7}{24}$ Ⓓ $\frac{7}{12}$

1 Which fraction is a multiple of $\frac{1}{5}$?

Ⓐ $\frac{2}{6}$ Ⓒ $\frac{3}{5}$

Ⓑ $\frac{4}{8}$ Ⓓ $\frac{5}{2}$

---

2 Eliza is writing the multiples of the fraction $\frac{1}{4}$. She starts the list with $\frac{1}{4}$. What is the multiple she should write next?

---

3 Jeremy writes multiples of $\frac{1}{6}$. Which fractions are multiples he should have in his list?

Select **all** the correct answers.

Ⓐ $\frac{1}{12}$

Ⓑ $\frac{2}{6}$

Ⓒ $\frac{3}{8}$

Ⓓ $\frac{5}{6}$

Ⓔ $\frac{6}{5}$

---

4 Which fractions are multiples of $\frac{1}{8}$?

Place an X in the table to show if each fraction is a multiple of $\frac{1}{8}$ or not.

	Multiple of $\frac{1}{8}$	Not a Multiple of $\frac{1}{8}$
$\frac{2}{8}$		
$\frac{2}{16}$		
$\frac{4}{8}$		
$\frac{8}{8}$		

5 Gianna wrote the fractions $\frac{3}{12}$ and $\frac{6}{12}$ as multiples of the same fraction.

What fraction are they a multiple of?

Ⓐ $\frac{12}{1}$

Ⓑ $\frac{1}{2}$

Ⓒ $\frac{1}{4}$

Ⓓ $\frac{1}{12}$

6 Which expression is equal to $\frac{3}{8}$?

Ⓐ $\frac{1}{3} \times 8$

Ⓑ $\frac{1}{8} \times 3$

Ⓒ $\frac{3}{1} \times 8$

Ⓓ $\frac{8}{3} \times 1$

7 Lin made a list of multiples of $\frac{1}{10}$ in order from LEAST to GREATEST. Which three fractions come next in the list?

Fill in the blanks with the fractions to show the correct order of the list.

$\frac{5}{10}$, $\frac{6}{10}$, $\frac{7}{10}$, _____, _____, _____

$\frac{2}{10}$	$\frac{8}{10}$	$\frac{9}{10}$	$\frac{10}{10}$	$\frac{14}{20}$

8 Reggie wrote three fractions that are all multiples of a unit fraction.

$\frac{3}{5}$, $\frac{2}{5}$, $\frac{4}{5}$

Which fraction are these three fractions a multiple of?

Ⓐ $\frac{1}{5}$

Ⓑ $\frac{1}{4}$

Ⓒ $\frac{4}{10}$

Ⓓ $\frac{5}{1}$

9 Jason creates multiples of each fraction shown. What number did he multiply each fraction by to create the multiple?

$\frac{1}{3} \times$ _____ $= \frac{5}{3}$

$\frac{1}{8} \times$ _____ $= \frac{4}{8}$

$\frac{1}{6} \times$ _____ $= \frac{3}{6}$

10 Charlotte multiplies a fraction by 7 to get $\frac{7}{12}$. Which fraction did she multiply?

Ⓐ $\frac{1}{7}$

Ⓑ $\frac{1}{12}$

Ⓒ $\frac{7}{1}$

Ⓓ $\frac{12}{1}$

1 Carlos lives $\frac{3}{8}$ mile from his school. He walks to school each morning and gets a ride home after school. Which expression is used to find the number of miles Carlos walks in 5 days?

Ⓐ $3 \times \frac{1}{8}$

Ⓑ $5 \times \frac{1}{8}$

Ⓒ $1 \times \frac{3}{8}$

Ⓓ $5 \times \frac{3}{8}$

2 Marko runs $\frac{3}{5}$ miles 3 times a week. Which expression is equal to the distance Marko runs each week?

Ⓐ $3 \times \frac{1}{5}$

Ⓑ $6 \times \frac{1}{5}$

Ⓒ $9 \times \frac{1}{5}$

Ⓓ $15 \times \frac{1}{5}$

3 What number is needed to complete each equation?

$4 \times \frac{3}{5} = $ _____ $\times \frac{1}{5}$

$6 \times \frac{2}{3} = $ _____ $\times \frac{1}{3}$

$5 \times \frac{6}{5} = $ _____ $\times \frac{1}{5}$

4 Larry practices his guitar $\frac{5}{6}$ hour on 4 different days each week. Which expression shows the number of hours Larry practices each week?

Ⓐ $4 \times \frac{1}{6}$

Ⓑ $9 \times \frac{1}{6}$

Ⓒ $20 \times \frac{1}{6}$

Ⓓ $24 \times \frac{1}{6}$

5 Donna buys some fabric to make placemats. She makes 9 different placemats. She needs $\frac{1}{5}$ yard of fabric for each placemat.

What is the unknown number in the equation that represents how much fabric she needs?

$\frac{9}{5} = $ _____ $\times \frac{1}{5}$

6 Which of these equations are true? Select the **three** correct answers.

Ⓐ $2 \times \frac{7}{5} = 10 \times \frac{1}{5}$

Ⓑ $3 \times \frac{6}{5} = 9 \times \frac{1}{5}$

Ⓒ $4 \times \frac{5}{3} = 20 \times \frac{1}{3}$

Ⓓ $5 \times \frac{3}{4} = 15 \times \frac{1}{4}$

Ⓔ $6 \times \frac{3}{2} = 18 \times \frac{1}{2}$

7 Each of the fractions can be written as a product of a whole number and a fraction. What numbers correctly complete the equations?

Fill in the boxes with the correct numbers from the list. You will not use all the numbers.

$$\frac{7}{5} = \boxed{} \times \boxed{}$$

$$\frac{10}{5} = \boxed{} \times \boxed{}$$

$\frac{1}{5}$	$\frac{2}{5}$	$\frac{5}{5}$	5	7	10

---

8 What is the unknown number in the equation?

$$5 \times \frac{7}{12} = \boxed{} \times \frac{1}{12}$$

Ⓐ 12

Ⓑ 17

Ⓒ 35

Ⓓ 60

---

9 What numbers will correctly complete the equation?

$$4 \times \frac{3}{10} = \frac{\boxed{} \times \boxed{}}{10}$$

---

10 Which expression is equivalent to $2 \times \frac{3}{100}$?

Ⓐ $5 \times \frac{1}{100}$

Ⓑ $5 \times \frac{3}{100}$

Ⓒ $6 \times \frac{1}{100}$

Ⓓ $6 \times \frac{3}{100}$

© Houghton Mifflin Harcourt Publishing Company

1 Jason's soccer practice lasts for $\frac{2}{3}$ hour. He goes to practice 5 days a week. How many hours does Jason spend at soccer practice each week?

(A) $7\frac{1}{2}$ hours

(B) $5\frac{2}{3}$ hours

(C) $4\frac{1}{3}$ hours

(D) $3\frac{1}{3}$ hours

2 Trevor paints sections of a fence. Each section is $\frac{7}{10}$ meter long. He has 5 more sections left to paint. What equation can Trevor use to find the length, l, of the fence he has already painted?

$l = $ ☐ ☐ ☐

| + | 3 | $\frac{9}{10}$ | × | 8 | $\frac{1}{10}$ |

3 Mrs. Tokala uses $\frac{9}{10}$ of a can of coffee beans each week. How many cans of coffee beans does she use in 6 weeks?

(A) $\frac{9}{60}$

(B) $4\frac{5}{10}$

(C) $5\frac{4}{10}$

(D) $6\frac{9}{10}$

4 Maddie makes a batch of popcorn balls. She uses $\frac{3}{4}$ cup of raisins. She uses 5 times as much popcorn as raisins.

How many cups of popcorn does Maddie need?

_____

5 Mr. Tuyen uses $\frac{5}{8}$ of a tank of gas each week to drive to and from his job. How many tanks of gas does Mr. Tuyen use in 7 weeks?

(A) $1\frac{4}{8}$

(B) $3\frac{5}{8}$

(C) $4\frac{3}{8}$

(D) $7\frac{5}{8}$

6 Mimi recorded a play that lasted $\frac{2}{3}$ hour. She watched it 3 times over the weekend to study the lines.

How many hours did Mimi spend watching the play?

(A) 2

(B) $2\frac{1}{3}$

(C) 3

(D) $3\frac{2}{3}$

Name _____

7 Rudi is comparing shark lengths. Shark A is $4\frac{1}{2}$ feet long. Shark B is 3 times as long as shark A. She draws a bar model to show this information.

Shark A

Shark B

Fill in the blanks with the correct answers from the list to complete the statements.

Each block in the model equals

_____ feet.

The length of shark B is

_____ feet.

$1\frac{1}{2}$	3	$4\frac{1}{2}$	$7\frac{1}{2}$	$13\frac{1}{2}$

8 Mrs. McGlashan is making paint for her class. She needs $\frac{3}{4}$ cup of water for each batch. Mrs. McGlashan has a 1-cup measuring cup that has no other markings. Which number of batches of paint can she make using only the 1-cup measuring cup?

Ⓐ 10   Ⓒ 6

Ⓑ 8   Ⓓ 5

9 Tamal used $\frac{7}{8}$ bag of soil for his vegetable garden. He used 6 times as much soil for his flower garden.

How many bags of soil did Tamal use for his flower garden?

_____

10 Hannah is baking 3 batches of health bars. She needs $\frac{2}{3}$ cup of carob chips for each batch of bars. Hannah completed the equations shown to find the number of cups of carob chips she needs to make 3 batches.

$3 \times \frac{2}{3} = \frac{9}{3}$ and $\frac{9}{3} = 3$

Why is Hannah incorrect?

Ⓐ Hannah is not correct because $3 \times \frac{2}{3} = \frac{11}{3}$

Ⓑ Hannah is not correct because $3 \times \frac{2}{3} = \frac{5}{3}$

Ⓒ Hannah is not correct because $3 \times \frac{2}{3} = \frac{6}{3}$

Ⓓ Hannah is not correct because $3 \times \frac{2}{3} = \frac{6}{9}$

1 Mateo walks $\frac{4}{10}$ of a mile to Zack's house. What is the distance to Zack's house as a fraction in hundredths?

(A) $\frac{1}{40}$ (C) $\frac{40}{100}$

(B) $\frac{4}{100}$ (D) $\frac{100}{4}$

---

2 Jessie added $\frac{5}{10} + \frac{25}{100}$. What sum did she get?

$\frac{\boxed{}}{\boxed{}}$

---

3 Carlos completed the following number sentence.

$\frac{6}{10} + \underline{} = \frac{80}{100}$

Which fraction did he write for the unknown addend?

(A) $\frac{20}{10}$ (C) $\frac{2}{100}$

(B) $\frac{74}{100}$ (D) $\frac{20}{100}$

---

4 Julian is building a birdhouse. The house is $\frac{25}{100}$ meter high without the roof. The roof is $\frac{2}{10}$ meter high. What is the height of the birdhouse with the roof?

Fill in the blanks with the correct answers from the list.

$\underline{} + \underline{} = \underline{}$

$\frac{2}{100}$	$\frac{20}{100}$	$\frac{25}{100}$	$\frac{27}{100}$	$\frac{45}{100}$	$\frac{100}{20}$

---

5 Complete this equation.

$\frac{6}{10} + \frac{x}{100} = \frac{87}{100}$

(A) $x = 17$ (C) $x = 51$

(B) $x = 27$ (D) $x = 81$

Name _____

6 Which fraction is equivalent to $\frac{90}{100}$?

  Ⓐ $\frac{9}{100}$ Ⓒ $\frac{90}{10}$

  Ⓑ $\frac{9}{10}$ Ⓓ $\frac{900}{100}$

7 Emily checked to see if the fractions were equivalent.

Place an X in the table to show if they are equivalent or not.

	Equivalent	Not Equivalent
$\frac{3}{10} = \frac{3}{1}$		
$\frac{5}{10} = \frac{50}{100}$		
$\frac{7}{10} = \frac{1}{7}$		
$\frac{1}{10} = \frac{10}{100}$		

8 Roberto walked $\frac{6}{10}$ mile to his friend's house. Together, they walked $\frac{25}{100}$ mile to school. How far did Roberto walk?

  Ⓐ $\frac{31}{100}$ mile   Ⓒ $\frac{85}{100}$ mile

  Ⓑ $\frac{35}{100}$ mile   Ⓓ $\frac{95}{100}$ mile

9 Brian added a fraction to $\frac{3}{10}$ to get an answer of $\frac{45}{100}$.

What fraction did he add to $\frac{3}{10}$?

$\boxed{}$
$\boxed{}$

10 James tossed a coin $\frac{1}{10}$ meter as part of an experiment. He then tossed it $\frac{75}{100}$ meter during the second part of the experiment.

What was the combined distance he tossed the coin?

  Ⓐ $\frac{76}{100}$

  Ⓑ $\frac{76}{1000}$

  Ⓒ $\frac{85}{10}$

  Ⓓ $\frac{85}{100}$

1 What is $\frac{67}{100}$ in decimal form?

Ⓐ 0.67

Ⓑ 6.7

Ⓒ 67

Ⓓ 670

2 What is $2\frac{77}{100}$ written as a decimal?

_____

3 What is a fraction that is equivalent to 0.2?

Select the **two** correct answers.

Ⓐ $\frac{2}{10}$

Ⓑ $\frac{20}{10}$

Ⓒ $\frac{10}{2}$

Ⓓ $\frac{2}{100}$

Ⓔ $\frac{20}{100}$

4 Which of these equations is correct?

Ⓐ $\frac{27}{100} = 2.7$

Ⓑ $4.81 = 4\frac{81}{10}$

Ⓒ $\frac{63}{10} = 6.3$

Ⓓ $0.59 = \frac{59}{10}$

5 What is $3\frac{54}{100}$ written in decimal form?

Ⓐ 0.354

Ⓑ 3.54

Ⓒ 35.4

Ⓓ 354

6 How can the number $12\frac{20}{100}$ be written in decimal form?

Select the **two** correct answers.

Ⓐ 0.122

Ⓑ 1.22

Ⓒ 12.2

Ⓓ 12.02

Ⓔ 12.20

7 How can each of the fractions be written in decimal form?

Fill in the blanks with the correct answer.

$\frac{85}{100} =$ _____

$\frac{47}{10} =$ _____

$5\frac{2}{10} =$ _____

8 What is the unknown number in the equation?

$$\frac{\boxed{}}{100} = 0.47$$

Ⓐ 0.47

Ⓑ 4.7

Ⓒ 47

Ⓓ 470

9 Plot and label each fraction from the list at the correct location on the number line.

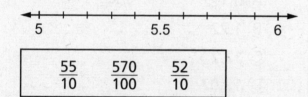

| $\frac{55}{10}$ | $\frac{570}{100}$ | $\frac{52}{10}$ |

10 Which of these equations are correct?

Select **all** the correct equations.

Ⓐ $\frac{42}{10} = 4.2$

Ⓑ $\frac{51}{100} = 5.1$

Ⓒ $0.75 = \frac{75}{10}$

Ⓓ $2.32 = 2\frac{32}{100}$

Ⓔ $6.78 = 6\frac{78}{10}$

11 Where are the numbers $2\frac{4}{10}$ and $2\frac{70}{100}$ located on a number line?

Plot and label the points on the number line to show where the numbers are located.

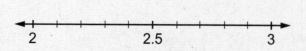

1 The top four results for a long jump competition at a track and field meet are shown.

Long Jump Results

Athlete	Distance
Ashton	4.56 m
Josey	4.29 m
Myrna	4.70 m
Sheniya	4.58 m

Who won the competition with the longest jump?

Ⓐ Ashton

Ⓑ Josey

Ⓒ Myrna

Ⓓ Sheniya

2 Arianna writes a decimal that is greater than 2.6 and less than 2.85. Which of these could be the decimal that Arianna writes?

Select **all** the correct answers.

Ⓐ 2.89

Ⓑ 2.8

Ⓒ 2.73

Ⓓ 2.60

Ⓔ 2.57

3 Place an X in the table to show whether each comparison is true or false.

	True	False
0.2 > 0.25		
4.8 > 4.08		
0.13 = 0.31		
3.4 < 3.40		

4 Which symbol correctly compares these numbers?

Fill in the blanks with the correct symbols from the list.

3.6 _____ 3.60

2.17 _____ 2.71

5.46 _____ 5.39

<	>	=

5 Maggie's teacher wrote a comparison on the board, but one of the numbers was erased by accident.

6.25 < 6.☐9

What numbers would correctly complete the inequality?

Select **all** the correct answers.

Ⓐ 0   Ⓓ 3

Ⓑ 1   Ⓔ 7

Ⓒ 2

Name _____

6 Matthew's fitness tracker says he ran 1.34 miles. Jack's fitness tracker says he ran 1.27 miles. Who ran the greater distance?

Ⓐ Jack, because 7 > 3

Ⓑ Jack, because 7 > 4

Ⓒ Matthew, because 3 > 2

Ⓓ Matthew, because 4 > 2

7 Which comparisons are true?

Select **all** the correct answers.

Ⓐ 0.21 < 0.27

Ⓑ 0.4 > 0.45

Ⓒ 0.21 > 3.20

Ⓓ 1.9 < 1.90

Ⓔ 6.2 > 6.02

8 Dylan's friends measured their heights in meters and recorded the results.

Heights

Abby	1.34 m
Bailey	1.26 m
Calvin	1.43 m
Dylan	1.47 m

How do their heights compare?

Write the names in the boxes in order from TALLEST on the top to SHORTEST on the bottom.

Abby		
Bailey		
Calvin		
Dylan		

9 Gene lives 0.6 mile from school. Kate lives 0.51 mile from school. Which statement correctly explains who lives closer to school?

Ⓐ Kate is closer, because 5 tenths is less than 6 tenths.

Ⓑ Gene is closer, because 6 tenths is greater than 5 tenths.

Ⓒ Kate is closer, because 1 hundredth is less than 6 hundredths.

Ⓓ Gene is closer, because 0 hundredths is less than 1 hundredth.

1 Mrs. DeMarco estimates the height of her garage door by comparing it to another object.

Which is the BEST object for her to use to estimate the height?

Ⓐ the width of a paper clip

Ⓑ the length of a baseball bat

Ⓒ the height of a license plate

Ⓓ the distance she can walk in two minutes

2 Greg wants to determine which liquid measures are equal.

Place an X in the table to show if the measurements are equal or not equal.

	Equal	Not equal
1 gallon = 6 pints		
1 pint = 2 cups		
1 quart = 2 pints		
1 cup = 4 quarts		
1 gallon = 4 quarts		

3 Kara adds 1 foot plus 24 inches and gets a total. Then, she determines which measurement is the same as this total. Which measurements are the same as this total? Select **all** that apply.

Ⓐ 1 yard

Ⓑ 2 yards

Ⓒ 3 feet

Ⓓ 6 feet

Ⓔ 36 inches

Ⓕ 48 inches

4 Which of the following measurements is the same as 30 minutes?

Ⓐ one-half hour

Ⓑ one hour

Ⓒ one and one-half hours

Ⓓ two hours

5 Theo needs a drop of food coloring for a science experiment. Fill in the blank with the correct answer from the list to complete the sentence about measuring a drop of food coloring.

A drop of food coloring equals about _____.

| 1 liter | 1 meter | 1 milliliter | 1 millimeter |

6 A veterinarian weighs a young puppy and notices that she weighs 3 pounds. How many ounces does this puppy weigh?

Ⓐ 30 ounces

Ⓑ 36 ounces

Ⓒ 48 ounces

Ⓓ 64 ounces

7 Mark's family has lived in the same town for exactly 3 years. How many months has he lived in this town?

Ⓐ 24 months

Ⓑ 30 months

Ⓒ 32 months

Ⓓ 36 months

8 George is making a list to show equivalent metric lengths.

Fill in the blanks with the correct metric equivalent.

2 meters = _____ millimeters

4 meters = _____ centimeters

7 centimeters = _____ millimeters

3 kilometers = _____ meters

9 Kylie threw a football 30 yards in a game. How many feet did she throw the football?

Ⓐ 90 feet

Ⓑ 180 feet

Ⓒ 300 feet

Ⓓ 1,080 feet

10 Ming wants to arrange the following metric units of length in order from LEAST to GREATEST.

Fill in the blanks with the correct answers from the list to put them in order from LEAST to GREATEST.

Least **Greatest**

[ ] , [ ] , [ ] , [ ]

2,000 m   3 km   800,000 cm   1,000,000 mm

1 Patrick mixed 3 quarts and 1 pint of orange juice with 3 pints of cranberry juice and 1 pint of grape juice to make punch. How much punch does he have?

(A) 4 quarts

(B) 4 quarts and 1 pint

(C) 5 quarts

(D) 5 quarts and 1 pint

2 An author signed books at a bookstore starting at 1:30 p.m. She signed books for 1 hour and 25 minutes.

At what time did the author stop signing books?

(A) 3:55

(B) 2:55

(C) 2:45

(D) 1:55

3 Wendy put 1 kilogram of apples, 375 grams of grapes, and 375 grams of oranges in a salad. What is the total mass of Wendy's salad?

(A) 1,250 grams

(B) 1,750 grams

(C) 1,740 grams

(D) 1,650 grams

4 Kyle is practicing for a 3-mile race. His normal time is 23 minutes and 26 seconds. Yesterday it took him only 21 minutes and 38 seconds.

How much faster was Kyle's time yesterday than his normal time?

_____ minute(s) and
_____ second(s)

5 After selling some old books and toys, Gwen and her brother Max had 5 one-dollar bills, 6 quarters, and 8 dimes. They agreed to divide the money equally.

What is the amount of money that Gwen and Max each earned?

(A) $3.40

(B) $3.65

(C) $7.15

(D) $7.30

6 Tran has $5.82. He is saving for a video game that costs $9.00.

How much more money does Tran need to buy the game?

(A) $3.18

(B) $3.28

(C) $13.82

(D) $14.82

7 Kylee, Gia, and Max each buy a ticket for the museum. Each ticket costs $7.75. What is the total cost of the tickets?

$ _____

8 Sandy cut three pieces of yarn to use for her art project. One piece was 1 foot 8 inches long, one was 10 inches long, and one was 2 feet 6 inches long.

How much yarn did Sandy use?

Ⓐ 40 inches

Ⓑ 50 inches

Ⓒ 60 inches

Ⓓ 68 inches

9 Rita is running a race and starts at the $1\frac{1}{2}$ mile mark. She runs $1\frac{1}{2}$ miles. At what mile mark does she finish?

Graph the total distance Rita runs on the number line.

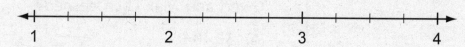

10 A bus left for the nature center at 9:15 a.m. The trip there took 1 hour and 45 minutes. What time did the bus arrive at the nature center?

Ⓐ 10:00 a.m.

Ⓑ 10:15 a.m.

Ⓒ 10:45 a.m.

Ⓓ 11:00 a.m.

1 Select **all** the rectangles with the given dimensions that would have a perimeter of 60 inches.

Ⓐ **length:** 12 inches   **width:** 5 inches

Ⓑ **length:** 15 inches   **width:** 15 inches

Ⓒ **length:** 20 inches   **width:** 10 inches

Ⓓ **length:** 27 inches   **width:** 3 inches

Ⓔ **length:** 30 inches   **width:** 2 inches

2 Emily made a design using a small square, a medium square, and a large square. She shaded the small square and the outer region.

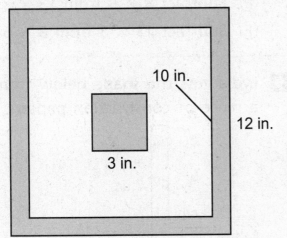

What is the area of the shaded part of the design in square inches?

_____

3 The lunchroom at Diane's school has a perimeter of 300 feet. The width of the lunchroom is 85 feet. What is the length of the lunchroom in feet?

Ⓐ 50   Ⓒ 75

Ⓑ 65   Ⓓ 150

4 Karlie painted a portrait. The height of the portrait is 14 inches. The width is half as long as the length. What is the area of the portrait in square inches?

_____

5 Patrick drew this plan for a new walkway through his backyard.

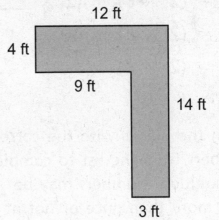

How many square feet of bricks will Patrick need to cover the walkway?

Ⓐ 168   Ⓒ 78

Ⓑ 90   Ⓓ 52

6 Joseph's notebook cover is 12 inches by 8 inches. He puts a wildlife sticker on the notebook cover. The sticker is 3 inches by 2 inches. How many square inches of the notebook cover are still showing?

Ⓐ 102

Ⓑ 96

Ⓒ 90

Ⓓ 84

7 Wilma used 60 centimeters of lace to make a border around a rectangular card. The width of the card is 20 centimeters. What is the length of the card?

$$P = (2 \times \ell) \, (2 \times W)$$

$$\underline{\quad} = (2 \times \ell) + (2 \times \underline{\quad})$$

$$\underline{\quad} = (2 \times \ell) + 40$$

$$20 = (2 \times \ell)$$

$$\underline{\quad} = \ell$$

Fill in the blanks with the correct numbers from the list to complete the solution. Numbers may be used more than once or not at all.

| 10 | 15 | 20 | 30 | 40 | 60 |

8 One wall of Patel's bedroom is 13 feet wide and 8 feet tall. A window on the wall is 3 feet high and 6 feet long. Which statements tell how to find the amount of wallpaper Patel would need to cover this wall?

Select **all** the correct answers.

Ⓐ Add 13 + 8 + 3 + 6.

Ⓑ Add 13 × 8 and 3 × 6.

Ⓒ Subtract 18 from 13 × 8.

Ⓓ Subtract 3 × 6 from 13 × 8.

Ⓔ Subtract 8 × 6 from 13 × 3

Ⓕ Subtract 13 × 8 from 3 × 6.

9 Lydia cuts the shape below from a piece of construction paper.

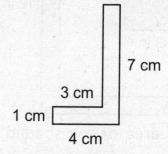

Select **all** the products Lydia can add to find the area of the shape in square centimeters.

Ⓐ 1 × 3 and 7 × 1

Ⓑ 3 × 1 and 6 × 1

Ⓒ 4 × 1 and 6 × 1

Ⓓ 7 × 4 and 3 × 1

Ⓔ 7 × 1 and 4 × 1

1 James reads a book for school for one week. He keeps track of his time. He made this line plot to show how many days he reads the book for the different lengths of time.

**Length of Time Reading
During a Week (in hours)**

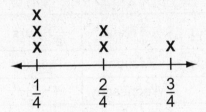

How much total time did James read?

Ⓐ 2 hours Ⓑ $2\frac{1}{4}$ hours Ⓒ $2\frac{2}{4}$ hours Ⓓ $2\frac{3}{4}$ hours

2 Carlos is looking at a line plot showing the length of the shadows of seven flowers.

Length of Shadows (in meters)

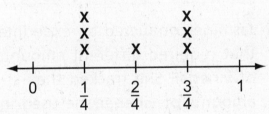

Place an X in the table to show if each statement is true or false.

	True	False
No flowers have a shadow that is $\frac{4}{4}$ meters long.		
An equal amount of flowers have a shadow that is $\frac{1}{4}$ of a meter and $\frac{3}{4}$ of a meter long.		
The total length of all of the shadows is greater than 4 meters.		
The difference between the longest and shortest shadow is $\frac{3}{4}$ of a meter.		

3 Esme collected coins in several jars. The line plot shows the weight of the coins in each jar.

Jars of Coins

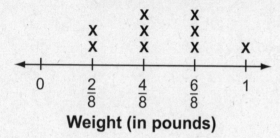

Weight (in pounds)

How many pounds of coins did Esme collect?

(A) $3\frac{7}{8}$ pounds   (C) $5\frac{7}{8}$ pounds

(B) $4\frac{7}{8}$ pounds   (D) 6 pounds

4 Leah does her homework each day after school. The data show the lengths of time Leah studied during the past 2 weeks.

Lengths of studying in hours:

$\frac{2}{4}, \frac{2}{4}, \frac{3}{4}, \frac{3}{4}, \frac{1}{4}, 1, \frac{3}{4}, \frac{3}{4}, 1, \frac{2}{4}$

Draw Xs on the line plot to represent the lengths of time Leah studied.

Study Time

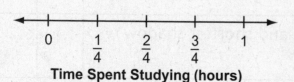

Time Spent Studying (hours)

5 Kevin is making a line plot to track the amount of time he practices his guitar in one week. The data for this week are in the table.

Practicing Guitar

$\frac{1}{2}$ Hour	$\frac{2}{2}$ Hour	$\frac{3}{2}$ Hours
Sunday	Monday	Tuesday
	Wednesday	Friday
	Thursday	
	Saturday	

How many Xs should be in the $\frac{1}{2}$ hour column of his line plot?

(A) 1   (C) 4

(B) 2   (D) 7

6 Jasmine conducted an experiment that required different amounts of vinegar. She tracked the amounts of vinegar she used in the line plot.

Amounts of Vinegar Used in Experiments (in cups)

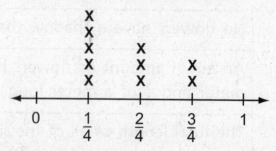

How many total cups of vinegar did Jasmine use?

1 How many degrees are in an
angle that turns through $\frac{1}{2}$ of
a circle?

(A) 45°

(B) 90°

(C) 180°

(D) 360°

2 An angle represents $\frac{1}{10}$ of a circle.
Show how to find the measure of
the angle in degrees.

Fill in the boxes with the correct
answers.

$$\frac{1}{10} = \frac{1 \times \boxed{}}{10 \times \boxed{}} = \frac{\boxed{}}{360}$$

3 What fraction of a circle does
a 27° angle turn through?

(A) $\frac{27}{27}$ of a circle

(B) $\frac{27}{90}$ of a circle

(C) $\frac{27}{180}$ of a circle

(D) $\frac{27}{360}$ of a circle

4 An angle measures 51°. Through
what fraction of a circle does the
angle turn?

5 An angle is shown in the circle.

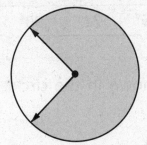

Which fraction represents the
unshaded angle in the figure?

(A) $\frac{90}{180}$

(B) $\frac{120}{180}$

(C) $\frac{90}{360}$

(D) $\frac{120}{360}$

6 How many degrees are in an
angle that turns through $\frac{1}{4}$ of
a circle?

(A) 90°

(B) 180°

(C) 270°

(D) 360°

7 Fill in the blanks with the correct answers from the list to complete the sentences.

An angle that turns through $\frac{1}{5}$ of a circle is a _____ angle.

An angle that turns through $\frac{1}{8}$ of a circle is a _____ angle.

36°	45°	72°	90°

8 An angle is shown in the circle.

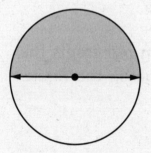

Which fraction represents the angle turn in the figure?

Ⓐ $\frac{1}{4}$ turn

Ⓑ $\frac{1}{2}$ turn

Ⓒ $\frac{3}{4}$ turn

Ⓓ $\frac{2}{2}$ turn

9 An angle represents $\frac{1}{12}$ of a circle. Show how to find the measure of the angle in degrees.

Fill in the boxes with the correct answers.

$$\frac{1}{12} = \frac{1 \times \boxed{}}{12 \times \boxed{}} = \frac{\boxed{}}{360}$$

10 How many degrees are in an angle that turns through $\frac{1}{3}$ of a circle?

Ⓐ 90°

Ⓑ 120°

Ⓒ 180°

Ⓓ 360°

Name _____

1 Bryan sets an analog clock by turning the minute hand through 6 one-degree angles.

Through how many degrees does Bryan turn the minute hand?

Ⓐ 5
Ⓑ 6
Ⓒ 7
Ⓓ 60

2 A carousel turns counterclockwise, in one-degree sections, a total of 280 times.

What is the total number of degrees the carousel turns?

The carousel turns a total

of _____ degrees.

3 Mr. Ayles turns his steering wheel 56° to the right to steer around a curve.

Through how many one-degree angles does Mr. Ayles turn his steering wheel?

Ⓐ 1
Ⓑ 55
Ⓒ 56
Ⓓ 304

4 Marco tightens a bolt by turning a wrench in one-degree sections a total of 14 times.

What is the measure of the angle through which Marco turns the wrench?

Ⓐ 1 degree
Ⓑ 13 degrees
Ⓒ 14 degrees
Ⓓ 15 degrees

5 The windshield wiper on Jack's car sweeps to an 80° angle as it moves from the bottom of the windshield to the top.

Through how many one-degree angles does the windshield wiper turn?

Ⓐ 1
Ⓑ 80
Ⓒ 100
Ⓓ 360

6 A gear in a watch turns clockwise, in one-degree sections, a total of 300 times.

What is the total number of degrees the gear turns?

The gear turns a total of _____ degrees.

7 Mark an X in the table to show whether each angle turns through fewer than 10 or more than 10 one-degree angles.

	Fewer than 10	More than 10
15°		
9°		
12°		

---

8 Maggie drew this angle.

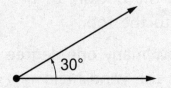

Fill in the blanks with the correct numbers from the list to complete the sentence. Numbers may be used more than once or not at all.

The angle measures _____ degrees because it turns through

_____ _____-degree angles.

1	29	30	31

9 Sam checked an astronomy table and learned that, on a particular day, the sun's position in the sky appeared to move through an angle of 11° in the first hour after sunrise.

By how many one-degree angles did the sun's position in the sky appear to turn in the first hour after sunrise?

Ⓐ 1   Ⓒ 12

Ⓑ 11   Ⓓ 60

---

10 A lawn sprinkler turns in one-degree sections a total of 135 times. What is the measure of the angle through which the sprinkler turns?

Ⓐ 1°   Ⓒ 45°

Ⓑ 35°   Ⓓ 135°

1 Use the protractor to measure
the angle.

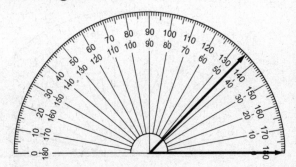

What is the measure of this
angle?

Ⓐ 30°

Ⓑ 45°

Ⓒ 60°

Ⓓ 90°

2 Use the protractor to measure
the angle.

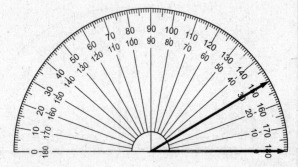

What is the measure of
the angle?

Ⓐ 30°

Ⓑ 60°

Ⓒ 120°

Ⓓ 150°

3 Use the protractor to measure
the angle.

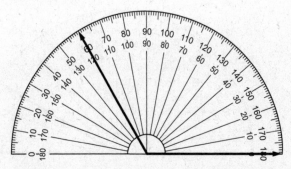

What is the measure of the
angle?

Ⓐ 60°

Ⓑ 80°

Ⓒ 120°

Ⓓ 130°

4 Fill in the blanks with the word
and angle measure from the list
to complete the sentence.

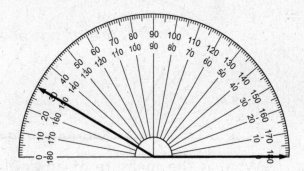

The angle shown is a(n) _____
angle because it measures _____.

acute	obtuse		right
90°	120°	150°	180°

5 Use the protractor to measure the angle.

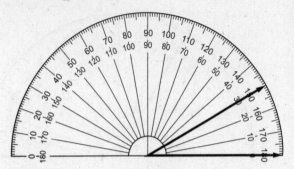

What is the measure of an angle whose measure is 30° greater than the angle shown?

(A) 30°

(B) 45°

(C) 60°

(D) 90°

6 Use the protractor to measure the angle.

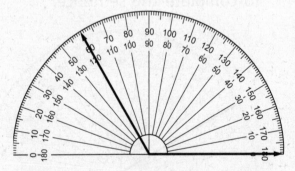

What is the measure of an angle whose measure is 20° less than the measure of the angle shown?

(A) 60°

(B) 90°

(C) 120°

(D) 140°

7 Use the protractor to measure the angle.

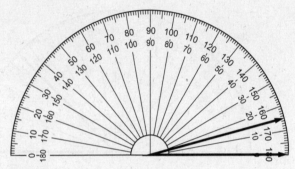

What is the measure of the angle?

(A) 15°

(B) 25°

(C) 35°

(D) 45°

8 Use the protractor to measure the angle.

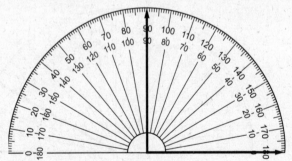

What is the measure of the angle?

(A) 0°

(B) 45°

(C) 90°

(D) 180°

1 What is the measure of the
unknown angle in the figure?

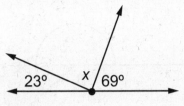

Ⓐ 46°

Ⓑ 88°

Ⓒ 92°

Ⓓ 180°

2 Nina drew the figure shown.

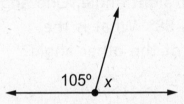

Place an X in the table to
show whether each statement
is true or false.

	True	False
The measure of a straight angle is 360°.		
To find the measure of x, Nina can subtract 105 from 360°.		
The measure of x is 75°.		

3 Eric put two angles together to
form a straight angle. One angle
measures 115°.

What is the measure of the
other angle?

Ⓐ 65°   Ⓒ 95°

Ⓑ 75°   Ⓓ 95°

4 Use the numbers to write an
equation that can be used to find
the measure of the unknown
angle.

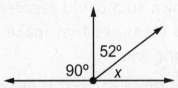

Fill in the blanks with the correct
numbers and symbol from the list
to complete the equation.

_____ + _____ + _____ = _____

| 38 | 52 | 90 | 180 | 142 | 360 | x |

5 What is the measure of the
unknown angle in the figure?

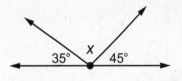

Ⓐ 80°   Ⓒ 100°

Ⓑ 90°   Ⓓ 180°

6 Jeffrey cuts a rectangle out of a piece of scrap paper as shown.

He wants to calculate the angle measure of the piece that is left over. Which equation can be used to solve for the angle x?

Ⓐ $x + 90 = 220$

Ⓑ $x - 90 = 220$

Ⓒ $180 - x = 220$

Ⓓ $220 - x = 180$

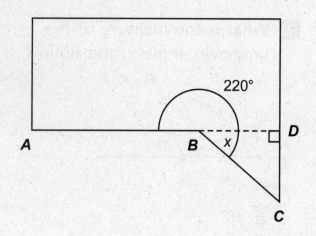

7 A straight line is divided into parts. Which sum could represent the angle measures that make up the straight line?

Select the **three** correct answers.

Ⓐ $120° + 60°$

Ⓑ $47° + 61° + 78°$

Ⓒ $15° + 40° + 53° + 72°$

Ⓓ $22° + 25° + 56° + 77°$

Ⓔ $10° + 15° + 17° + 22° + 26°$

8 Kayla drew this figure with a protractor.

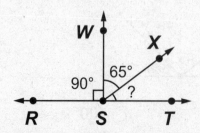

What is the measure of $\angle XST$?

$\angle XST =$ _____

9 Miko put two angles together to form a straight angle. One angle measures 88°. What is the measure of the other angle?

Ⓐ 42°   Ⓒ 82°

Ⓑ 72°   Ⓓ 92°

10 $\angle C$ and $\angle D$ form a straight line. Find the measure of $\angle D$ for each measure of $\angle C$ in the table below.

Write the correct angle measures from the list to complete the table.

Measure of $\angle C$	Measure of $\angle D$
122°	
35°	
62°	
105°	

58°	145°	118°	75°

1 Bella drew the figure below as an example for her classmate.

Which term describes the figure Bella drew?

Ⓐ ray

Ⓑ line

Ⓒ angle

Ⓓ line segment

2 Write each part of Figure A from the list in the correct place in the table.

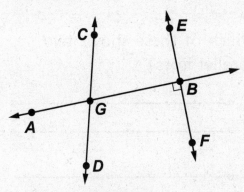

Figure A

Ray	Line	Line Segment

$\overline{EB}$ $\overleftrightarrow{AB}$ $\overrightarrow{GA}$ $\overrightarrow{BF}$

3 Tenley makes stained glass windows. She used this piece of stained glass in one of the windows.

How many right angles does this piece of stained glass appear to have?

Ⓐ 0

Ⓑ 1

Ⓒ 2

Ⓓ 3

4 Figure A is shown.

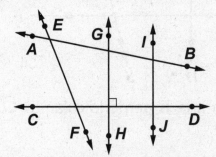

Place an X in the table to show whether the lines in Figure A are parallel or not.

	Parallel	Not Parallel
$\overleftrightarrow{GH}$ and $\overleftrightarrow{AB}$		
$\overleftrightarrow{IJ}$ and $\overleftrightarrow{GH}$		
$\overleftrightarrow{AB}$ and $\overleftrightarrow{CD}$		
$\overleftrightarrow{EF}$ and $\overleftrightarrow{IJ}$		

5 Julie drew the figure below as an example for her classmate.

Which of these terms BEST describes the figure Julie drew?

- Ⓐ ray
- Ⓑ line
- Ⓒ angle
- Ⓓ line segment

6 Look at the figure.

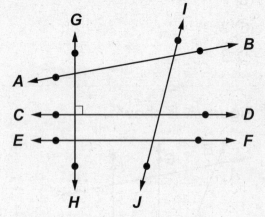

Which line is perpendicular to $\overleftrightarrow{CD}$?

- Ⓐ $\overleftrightarrow{AB}$
- Ⓑ $\overleftrightarrow{EF}$
- Ⓒ $\overleftrightarrow{GH}$
- Ⓓ $\overleftrightarrow{IJ}$

7 Which is the BEST name for this figure?

Which is the BEST name for this figure?

- Ⓐ line
- Ⓑ line segment
- Ⓒ ray
- Ⓓ angle

8 A quadrilateral is shown.

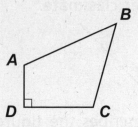

Place an X in the table to classify each angle.

	Acute	Obtuse	Right
∠A			
∠B			
∠C			
∠D			

9 Which of these shows two parallel lines?

Ⓐ

Ⓑ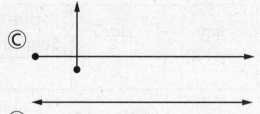

Ⓒ

Ⓓ

Name _____

1 A window is in the shape of a trapezoid with only 1 pair of parallel sides. Which figure could be the shape of the window?

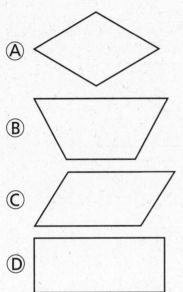

Ⓐ

Ⓑ

Ⓒ

Ⓓ

2 Write the correct letters in the table to classify the triangles.

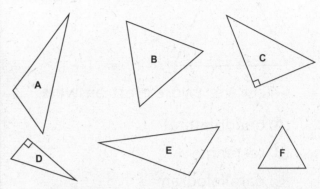

Acute Triangle	Obtuse Triangle	Right Triangle
__ __	__ __	__ __

A	B	C	D	E	F

3 Three shapes are given in the table below.

Place an X in the table to describe the sides and angles of each shape.

	2 Pairs of Parallel Sides	4 Equal Sides	4 Equal Angles
Square			
Trapezoid			
Rhombus			

4 A fish pond is in the shape of a rhombus. Which figure could be the shape of the fish pond?

Ⓐ

Ⓑ

Ⓒ

Ⓓ

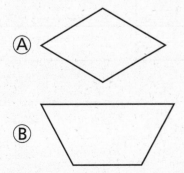

© Houghton Mifflin Harcourt Publishing Company

Grade 4 • Standards-Based Practice

65

Name _____

5 Classify the figure shown below.

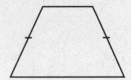

Select the **two** correct answers.

Ⓐ quadrilateral
Ⓑ rectangle
Ⓒ parallelogram
Ⓓ rhombus
Ⓔ trapezoid
Ⓕ square

6 A flag is in the shape of a right triangle. Which of the following could be the shape of the flag?

Ⓐ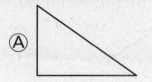

Ⓑ

Ⓒ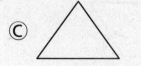

Ⓓ

7 Identify the number of right, acute, and obtuse angles there are in the given triangles in the table.

Fill in the blanks in the table with the correct answers.

Number of Angles

	Right Angle(s)	Acute Angle(s)	Obtuse Angle(s)
Right Triangle	_____	_____	_____
Acute Triangle	_____	_____	_____
Obtuse Triangle	_____	_____	_____

8 How many acute angles does an acute triangle have?

An acute triangle has _____ acute angles.

1 Jared drew the figure below.

How many lines of symmetry does the figure have?

Ⓐ 4   Ⓒ 2

Ⓑ 3   Ⓓ 1

2 Place an X in the table to show if each statement is always true, sometimes true, or never true.

	Always True	Sometimes True	Never True
A square has 4 lines of symmetry.			
A rhombus has 1 line of symmetry.			
A pentagon has 5 lines of symmetry.			
A scalene triangle has no lines of symmetry.			

3 Debbie leaves for her trip to San Diego on the 13th day of February. Since February is the second month, Debbie wrote the date as shown.

2/13

Debbie says all the numbers she wrote have a line symmetry. Is she correct?

Ⓐ yes, because she can fold the date to create two matching parts

Ⓑ no, because she cannot fold the date to create two matching parts

Ⓒ yes, because she can fold each number to create two matching parts

Ⓓ no, because she cannot fold the number 2 to create two matching parts

Name _____

4 Ethan uses shapes to write an equation that adds 2 shapes. Each shape stands for the number of lines of symmetry it has.

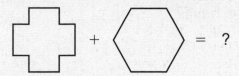

What is the sum?

_____

5 Andrew drew the figure below.

How many lines of symmetry does the figure have?

Ⓐ 4

Ⓑ 3

Ⓒ 2

Ⓓ 1

6 Brad drew the figure below.

How many lines of symmetry does the figure have?

Ⓐ 4

Ⓑ 3

Ⓒ 2

Ⓓ 1

7 Select the figure that has the greatest number of lines of symmetry.

Ⓐ rectangle

Ⓑ trapezoid

Ⓒ regular pentagon

Ⓓ equilateral triangle

8 Which line shows a line of symmetry for the pentagon?

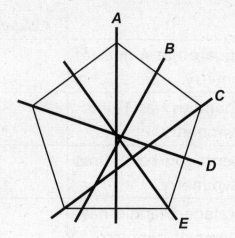

Select **all** the lines that are lines of symmetry.

Ⓐ A   Ⓓ D

Ⓑ B   Ⓔ E

Ⓒ C

9 How many lines of symmetry does the figure have?

_____

Practice Test

Item	Content Focus	DOK	Record
1	Apply the area and perimeter formulas for rectangles in problems.	2	
2	Investigate factors and multiples.	2	
3	Find quotients and remainders with 4-digit dividends and 1-digit divisors.	2	
4	Understand a fraction $\frac{a}{b}$ with $a > 1$ as a sum of fractions $\frac{1}{b}$.	2	
5	Recognize a digit in one place is ten times what it is in the place to its right.	1	
6	Compare two decimals to hundredths.	2	
7	Recognize angles and understand concepts of angle measurement.	1	
8	Write and solve problems with whole numbers using the four operations.	2	
9	Draw and identify points, lines, line segments, rays, angles (right, acute, obtuse), and perpendicular and parallel lines.	1	
10	Multiply 4-digit numbers by 1-digit numbers, and two 2-digit numbers.	2	
11	Add two fractions with respective denominators 10 and 100.	1	
12	Solve word problems involving distances, intervals of time, and money.	2	
13	Understand a fraction $\frac{a}{b}$ with $a > 1$ as a sum of fractions $\frac{1}{b}$.	2	
14	Write and solve problems with whole numbers using the four operations.	2	
15	Recognize and generate equivalent fractions.	3	
16	Use place value understanding to round multi-digit whole numbers.	1	
17	Interpret a multiplication equation as a comparison.	1	
18	Measure and sketch angles using a protractor.	2	
19	Express measurements in a larger unit in terms of a smaller unit.	1	
20	Classify 2-D figures based on the presence or absence of lines or angles.	2	
21	Add and subtract mixed numbers with like denominators.	1	
22	Use addition and subtraction to find unknown angles on a diagram.	2	
23	Identify line-symmetric figures and draw lines of symmetry.	2	
24	Add and subtract fractions by using information presented in line plots.	2	
25	Read, write, and compare multi-digit whole numbers.	2	
26	Fluently add and subtract multi-digit whole numbers.	1	
27	Multiply a fraction by a whole number.	2	
28	Solve word problems involving distances, intervals of time, and money.	2	
29	Multiply or divide to solve problems involving multiplicative comparison.	2	

Name

Item	Content Focus	DOK	Record
30	Find quotients and remainders with 4-digit dividends and 1-digit divisors.	2	
31	Compare two fractions with different numerators and denominators.	2	
32	Use decimal notation for fractions with denominators 10 or 100.	1	
33	Generate a number or shape pattern that follows a given rule.	2	
34	Write and solve problems using the four operations.	3	
35	Generate a number or shape pattern that follows a given rule.	3	
36	Multiply 4-digit numbers by 1-digit numbers and two 2-digit numbers.	3	
37	Understand a multiple of $\frac{a}{b}$ as a multiple of $\frac{1}{b}$.	3	
38	Multiply or divide to solve multiplicative comparison problems.	3	
39	Classify 2-D figures based on lines or angles.	3	

1 A rectangle has an area of 24 square inches. If the rectangle's width were 2 inches wider, its area would be 40 square inches. What is the length in inches of the rectangle?

Ⓐ 3   Ⓒ 12

Ⓑ 8   Ⓓ 16

2 Select **all** the composite numbers that are the product of two prime numbers.

Ⓐ 6   Ⓓ 27

Ⓑ 12   Ⓔ 45

Ⓒ 21   Ⓕ 51

3 A certain 3-digit number is divisible by 4. The digit in the hundreds place is divisible by 4, but the digit in the tens place is not.

Which of the following could be the 3-digit number?

Ⓐ 420   Ⓒ 618

Ⓑ 584   Ⓓ 863

4 Raven draws a model to show $\frac{3}{5} = \frac{1}{5} + \frac{1}{5} + \frac{1}{5}$. She draws a circle and divides it into equal sections. She shades some of the sections.

How many sections should Raven divide the circle into?

Ⓐ 3, because the numerator is 3

Ⓑ 5, because the numerator is 5

Ⓒ 3, because she is adding 3 fractions

Ⓓ 5, because each section shows $\frac{1}{5}$ of the whole

5 In which numbers is the value of the digit 2 equal to ten times the value of the digit 2 in 372,159?

Select **all** the correct answers.

Ⓐ 184,237

Ⓑ 215,149

Ⓒ 424,189

Ⓓ 512,099

Ⓔ 627,815

6 Which comparison is true?

Ⓐ 0.4 > 0.86

Ⓑ 0.43 > 0.8

Ⓒ 0.43 < 0.86

Ⓓ 0.68 < 0.34

7 Which of these is an angle?

Ⓐ

Ⓒ

Ⓑ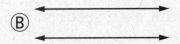

Ⓓ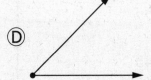

8 Rosalee bought 3 bracelets and 4 necklaces and spent between $60 and $80. Each bracelet costs the same amount. Each necklace costs the same amount. The price of a bracelet is $12.

Part A

What is the LEAST amount Rosalee could have spent on a necklace?

_____

Part B

What is the GREATEST amount Rosalee could have spent on a necklace?

_____

9 Place an X in the table to show if the attribute applies to the figure.

Contains acute angles		
Contains obtuse angles		
Contains perpendicular sides		

10 Which expression is equivalent to 46 × 29?

Ⓐ (40 × 2) + (40 × 9) + (6 × 2) + (6 × 9)

Ⓑ (4 × 20) + (4 × 9) + (6 × 20) + (6 × 9)

Ⓒ (40 × 2) + (40 × 90) + (6 × 2) + (6 × 90)

Ⓓ (40 × 20) + (40 × 9) + (6 × 20) + (6 × 9)

11 What is $\frac{2}{10} + \frac{7}{100}$?

Write the correct numbers from the list in the boxes in the equation. You will not use all the numbers.

$$\frac{2}{10} + \frac{7}{100} = \frac{\boxed{}}{100} + \frac{7}{100} = \frac{\boxed{}}{\boxed{}}$$

2	9	10	20	27	72	100

12 After school, Andrew boards the school bus and waits 5 minutes for the bus to leave school. The ride to Andrew's bus stop takes 23 minutes. It takes 4 minutes for Andrew to walk from the bus stop to his house. Andrew arrives home from school at 4:10 p.m.

At what time does Andrew board the school bus?

Ⓐ 3:28 p.m.

Ⓑ 3:33 p.m.

Ⓒ 3:38 p.m.

Ⓓ 3:56 p.m.

13 Will adds some fractions and correctly finds the sum of $\frac{5}{8}$.
Find **all** of the expressions equal to $\frac{5}{8}$.

Ⓐ $\frac{2}{8} + \frac{3}{8}$

Ⓑ $\frac{2}{8} + \frac{2}{8}$

Ⓒ $\frac{1}{8} + \frac{2}{8} + \frac{2}{8}$

Ⓓ $\frac{1}{8} + \frac{2}{8} + \frac{3}{8}$

Ⓔ $\frac{1}{8} + \frac{1}{8} + \frac{2}{8} + \frac{1}{8}$

14 What is the value of p in the equation?

$212 + 125 = 200 + p$

Enter the correct answer in the box.

$p = \boxed{}$

15 Valerie writes four fractions that are equivalent to $\frac{8}{12}$ and explains how she can use fraction strip models to show that the fractions are equivalent.

Place an X in the table to show the fraction matching Valerie's explanation.

	$\frac{2}{3}$	$\frac{4}{6}$	$\frac{16}{24}$	$\frac{32}{48}$
I divided each of the original parts into two equal parts.				
I divided each of the original parts into four equal parts.				
I combined two parts to make one larger part.				
I combined four parts to make one larger part.				

16 What is 624,379 rounded to the nearest ten thousand?

Ⓐ 620,000   Ⓒ 624,380

Ⓑ 624,000   Ⓓ 630,000

17 Hernan chooses two numbers. The first number is 30. He knows that 30 is 6 times the second number. What is the second number?

_____

18 What is the measure of the acute angle?

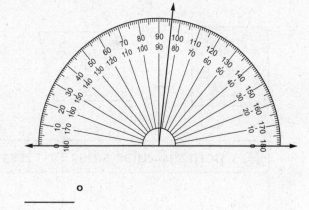

_____ °

19 A student created the following table to show how to change from centimeters to meters. Look at the centimeter value in the left column and determine which meter measurement it equals.

Write the correct numbers from the list in the table. You will not use all the numbers.

Centimeters	Meters
100	
200	
500	
1,000	

1	2	5	10	20	50	100

20 Write the letter for each shape under the correct description in the table. Some shapes may be used more than once.

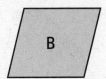

Has perpendicular sides	Has parallel sides	Has a right angle

21 Which of the following equations is true?

  Ⓐ 27 + 15 = 20 + 23

  Ⓑ 31 − 11 = 9 + 11 + 11

  Ⓒ 35 + 7 = 50 − 8

  Ⓓ 28 + 15 = 29 + 15

22 The diagram shows a right angle cut into two smaller angles. If angle *ABD* is 60°, what is the measurement of angle *DBC*?

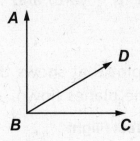

  Ⓐ 30°   Ⓒ 90°

  Ⓑ 60°   Ⓓ 150°

---

23 Select **all** the figures that show a line of symmetry.

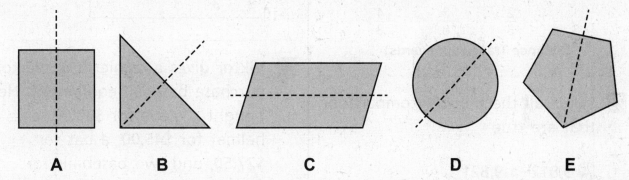

  A   **B**   **C**   **D**   **E**

  Ⓐ shape A

  Ⓑ shape B

  Ⓒ shape C

  Ⓓ shape D

  Ⓔ shape E

24 Ryan tests 10 different paper airplane designs and flies them in the school gym. He finds that 5 fly $\frac{1}{2}$ yard, 3 fly $\frac{1}{4}$ yard, and 2 fly $\frac{1}{8}$ yard.

Create a line plot that shows the distances of the planes flown.

Ryan's Test Flight

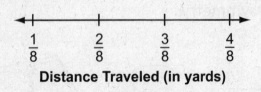

Distance Traveled (in yards)

25 Select **all** the number comparisons that are true.

Ⓐ 9,812 < 9,821

Ⓑ 7,153 > 7,315

Ⓒ 4,912 < 4,219

Ⓓ 6,741 > 6,417

Ⓔ 8,523 > 8,235

26 2,937 + 3,405 =

Ⓐ 5,342

Ⓒ 6,412

Ⓑ 6,342

Ⓓ 6,512

27 Maggie has 5 containers to plant flowers in. Each container holds $\frac{2}{3}$ cup of soil. How much total soil will Maggie use?

Fill in the blank with the correct number from the list.

Maggie will use a total of _____ cups of soil.

| $\frac{5}{3}$ | $\frac{7}{3}$ | $\frac{10}{3}$ | 3 | 4 |

28 Viktor gives a cashier $125.00 to purchase baseball equipment. He bought a glove for $30.00, a helmet for $45.00, a bat for $27.50, and two baseballs for $5.00 each. Viktor pays an additional $7.00 for tax. Viktor asks to get all of his change in quarters.

How many quarters does he get?

Ⓐ 12

Ⓒ 22

Ⓑ 21

Ⓓ 540

29 Sarah scored 132 points during basketball season. Her sister Jenny scored three times as many points during basketball season. Which equation shows how to determine the number of points Jenny scored in the season?

Ⓐ $y \div 3 = 132$

Ⓑ $132 - 3 = y$

Ⓒ $132 + 3 = y$

Ⓓ $3 \times y = 132$

30 What is 4,050 divided by 5?

Ⓐ 800   Ⓒ 811

Ⓑ 810   Ⓓ 851

31 Kiara is comparing five fractions to $\frac{1}{2}$. Which statements show an accurate comparison?

Select **all** the correct answers.

Ⓐ $\frac{1}{2} < \frac{3}{4}$

Ⓑ $\frac{1}{2} < \frac{2}{5}$

Ⓒ $\frac{1}{2} = \frac{3}{6}$

Ⓓ $\frac{1}{2} > \frac{5}{7}$

Ⓔ $\frac{1}{2} > \frac{2}{8}$

© Houghton Mifflin Harcourt Publishing Company

32 Esme is converting fractions to decimals. What does each fraction equal as a decimal?

Fill in the blanks with the correct numbers from the list.

$\frac{3}{10}$ = _____

$\frac{3}{100}$ = _____

$\frac{32}{100}$ = _____

| 0.23 | 0.03 | 3.00 | 0.32 | 0.30 | 3.02 |

33 Greg noticed a pattern in the following numbers:
2, 5, 11, 23 . . .

He wants to continue the pattern. What are the next three numbers?

2, 5, 11, 23, _____, _____, _____

34 Jenna takes 60 photos at her family reunion. She frames 18 of them. She arranges the remaining photos equally across 6 pages in her family's scrapbook.

• Write an equation that can be used to determine the number of photos, *p*, that Jenna arranges on each page of the scrapbook.

• Find the number of photos that Jenna arranges on each page.

• Explain how you can check the reasonableness of your answer.

35 Alex stores his baseball card collection in a soft sleeve album. The table below shows the total number of cards he has stored and the number of pages with cards.

Baseball Card Collection

Number of Pages	Number of Cards
3	18
7	42
11	66
15	90
19	?

- If the number of cards on each page is the same and the pattern continues, write a number sentence that could be used to find the total number of cards Alex stores on 19 pages.

- Find the total number of cards Alex stores on 19 pages.

- Based on the pattern, Alex's friend figures that Alex can store 24 cards on each page of his album. Explain the error in the friend's calculation. As part of your explanation, find the correct number of cards that Alex can store on each page of his album.

36 An apple farmer grows 4 different types of apples on her 36-acre farm. She grows 64 apple trees per acre.

- What is the total number of apple trees growing on her farm?

- If the farmer grows an equal number of trees for each type of apple, how many trees of each type does she grow?

37 The table shows the sizes and weights of packages of ground beef sold at a store.

Ground Beef

Size	Weight (in pounds)
Small	$\frac{2}{5}$
Medium	$\frac{4}{5}$
Large	$\frac{6}{5}$
Jumbo	$\frac{8}{5}$

- Joe bought 7 medium packages of ground beef and Anh bought 3 jumbo packages of ground beef. What is the difference in the weights, in pounds, of Joe's and Anh's purchases?

- Explain how you got your answer.

38 Patricia is buying peaches, oranges, apples, and plums for a fruit salad.

She buys 3 times as many peaches as oranges. She buys 2 times as many peaches as plums. She buys 4 oranges. How many peaches and plums does Patricia buy?

Patricia's recipe calls for 2 times as many apples as the rest of the fruit. How many apples does she need?

Use equations or drawings to explain how you got your answer.

39 Is this triangle best described as right, acute, or obtuse?

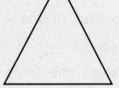

Explain how you know your answer is correct. Then explain why the other two choices are not correct.

1 The diagram shows the measurements of two rooms in a house.

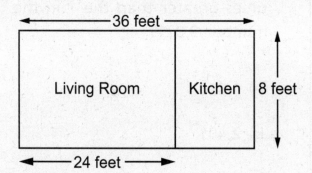

What is the area of the kitchen in square feet?

_____

2 Alison is helping set up 36 desks in rectangular rows for the classroom science fair. She has come up with three possible ways to arrange the desks. Which list could be the three desk arrangements?

(A) 3 rows of 12 desks
    4 rows of 8 desks
    9 rows of 6 desks

(C) 3 rows of 12 desks
    4 rows of 9 desks
    6 rows of 6 desks

(B) 3 rows of 6 desks
    2 rows of 18 desks
    6 rows of 5 desks

(D) 4 rows of 9 desks
    5 rows of 6 desks
    3 rows of 8 desks

3 Xavier is creating equivalent equations to solve $1{,}836 \div 3 = a$. What other equations could he create to solve this problem?

Select **all** the correct answers.

Ⓐ $3 \times a = 1{,}836$; $a = 612$

Ⓑ $1{,}836 - 3 = a$; $a = 1{,}833$

Ⓒ $1{,}836 - a = 3$; $a = 1{,}833$

Ⓓ $3 + a = 1{,}836$; $a = 1{,}839$

Ⓔ $3 + 1{,}836 = a$; $a = 1{,}839$

Ⓕ $1{,}836 \div a = 3$; $a = 612$

4 Which expressions have a sum of $\frac{4}{5}$?

Select **all** the correct answers.

Ⓐ $\frac{2}{5} + \frac{2}{5}$

Ⓑ $\frac{1}{5} + \frac{3}{5}$

Ⓒ $\frac{1}{5} + \frac{1}{5} + \frac{2}{5}$

Ⓓ $\frac{1}{5} + \frac{2}{5} + \frac{3}{5}$

Ⓔ $\frac{1}{5} + \frac{1}{5} + \frac{1}{5} + \frac{1}{5} + \frac{1}{5}$

5 Which number has a 1 that is ten times greater than the 1 in the number 9,021?

Ⓐ 1,820

Ⓑ 2,401

Ⓒ 4,713

Ⓓ 6,128

6 Which of these correctly compares the decimal numbers?

Ⓐ $0.03 > 0.06$

Ⓑ $0.10 < 0.03$

Ⓒ $0.13 < 0.17$

Ⓓ $0.10 > 0.17$

7 James wants to label the angles as either less than 90° or
between 90° and 180°

Place an X in the table to show which label is true for each angle.

	Less than 90°	Between 90° and 180°
A, B, C angle		
J, K, L angle		
R, S, T angle		

8 Janice raised money for a school fundraiser. The money was collected in
5 containers. The first 3 containers held exactly $15 apiece. The final
2 containers each held the same amount of money. Janice gathered a
total of $85. How much money was in each of the final 2 containers?

Ⓐ $15   Ⓒ $40

Ⓑ $20   Ⓓ $45

9 Which angle is obtuse?

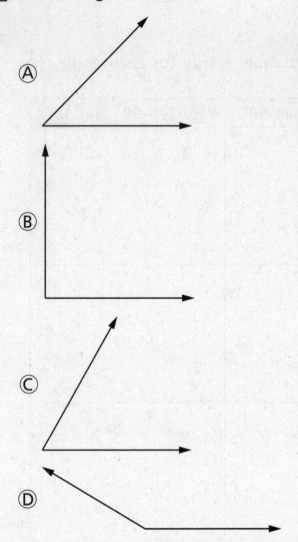

(A)

(B)

(C)

(D)

10 An area model is used to multiply two-digit numbers.

	10	+	3
20	200		60
+			
2	20		6

What problem is represented by the model?

_____ × 13 = _____

11 Which fraction is equivalent to $\frac{5}{10}$?

(A) $\frac{5}{1}$ (C) $\frac{50}{100}$

(B) $\frac{5}{100}$ (D) $\frac{50}{10}$

12 Seiji is making bread for a bake sale. The recipe calls for $\frac{3}{4}$ cup of butter for 1 loaf of bread. A stick of butter equals $\frac{1}{2}$ cup. How many sticks of butter will he need?

Fill in the blanks with the correct answers to complete the sentences.

Seiji will need a total of _____ sticks of butter for 2 loaves of bread.

Seiji will need a total of _____ sticks of butter for 4 loaves of bread.

1	2	3	4	5	6

13 Chan adds some fractions and correctly finds a sum of $\frac{6}{9}$.

Which expression shows the fractions that Chan added and equals $\frac{6}{9}$?

Ⓐ $\frac{2}{9} + \frac{3}{9}$

Ⓑ $\frac{2}{9} + \frac{2}{9} + \frac{1}{9}$

Ⓒ $\frac{1}{9} + \frac{2}{9} + \frac{3}{9}$

Ⓓ $\frac{1}{9} + \frac{1}{9} + \frac{2}{9} + \frac{3}{9}$

14 Given the value of the variable, which of the following equations are true?

Select **all** the correct answers.

Ⓐ $28 + 7 = 25 + n;\ n = 9$

Ⓑ $32 + 3 = 16 + y;\ y = 19$

Ⓒ $41 + 9 = m + 28;\ m = 12$

Ⓓ $51 + 11 = x + 50;\ x = 12$

Ⓔ $64 + 7 = 34 + z;\ z = 27$

Ⓕ $73 + 6 = 42 + k;\ k = 37$

15 Janelle created a number line to show equivalent fractions.

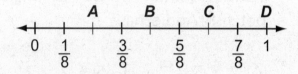

Which letters represent $\frac{1}{2}$ and $\frac{3}{4}$ on the number line?

Ⓐ The letter C is at $\frac{1}{2}$ and D is at $\frac{3}{4}$.

Ⓑ The letter B is at $\frac{1}{2}$ and C is at $\frac{3}{4}$.

Ⓒ The letter C is at $\frac{1}{2}$ and B is at $\frac{3}{4}$.

Ⓓ The letter B is at $\frac{1}{2}$ and D is at $\frac{3}{4}$.

16 Dennis is rounding numbers in a table to the nearest thousand.

Fill in the table with the correct answers.

Number	Rounded to Nearest Thousand
2,796	
3,470	
17,520	

17 Katie has 2 pet fish. Addie has 5 times as many pet fish as Katie. Which equation shows how many pet fish Addie has?

Ⓐ $2 \times 5 = ?$　　Ⓒ $5 + 2 = ?$

Ⓑ $2 + 5 = ?$　　Ⓓ $5 - 2 = ?$

18 Jeremy drew an angle that is 30° greater than a right angle. Which angle did he draw?

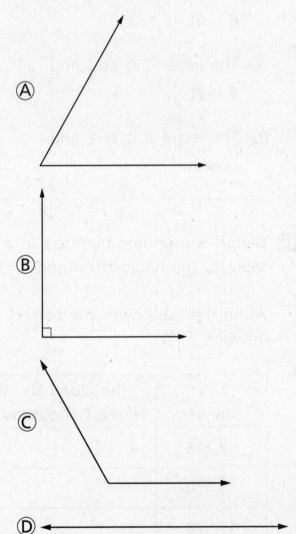

Ⓐ

Ⓑ

Ⓒ

Ⓓ

19 Bruce is 6 feet tall. How many inches tall is Bruce?

Ⓐ 18　　　Ⓒ 60

Ⓑ 48　　　Ⓓ 72

20 Figures are placed into two groups in a table.

Group 1	Group 2

Which attribute was used to sort the figures?

Ⓐ number of sides

Ⓑ number of angles

Ⓒ parallel sides

Ⓓ perpendicular sides

21 A bookstore sells 410 books in week 1 and 336 books in week 2. The manager sets a goal to sell the same number of books as the first 2 weeks for weeks 3 and 4.

If the store sells 425 books in week 3, how many books does the store need to sell in week 4 to meet the goal?

_____

22 The figure shows several angles with given measures and one unknown angle.

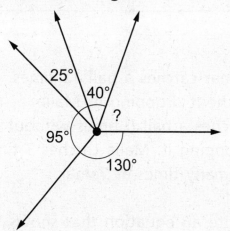

What is the measure of the unknown angle?

Fill in the blanks to complete the equation and the sentence.

$360 = ? +$ _____.
The measure of the unknown angle is _____°.

23 Which figure has exactly 4 lines of symmetry?

Ⓐ square

Ⓑ rectangle

Ⓒ pentagon

Ⓓ equilateral triangle

24 The students in Sarah's class measured their pencils to the nearest $\frac{1}{4}$ inch. They made a line plot to show the data.

Pencil Lengths

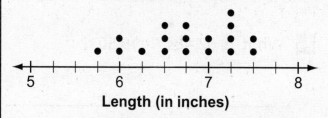

Length (in inches)

What is the difference between the longest pencil and the shortest pencil?

Ⓐ $1\frac{1}{2}$ inches

Ⓑ $1\frac{3}{4}$ inches

Ⓒ $2\frac{1}{4}$ inches

Ⓓ $2\frac{3}{4}$ inches

25 Danny uses the digits 3, 5, 6, and 8 to write a four-digit number. His number is greater than 5,683 but less than 6,538.

Which could be the number Danny writes?

Ⓐ six thousand three hundred fifty-eight

Ⓑ six thousand eight hundred thirty-five

Ⓒ five thousand six hundred eighty-three

Ⓓ five thousand three hundred sixty-eight

26 What is 62,484 + 19,503?

_____

27 Madison fills a $\frac{2}{3}$-cup measuring cup 4 times with water.

Which expression can Madison use to find the total amount of water in cups that she measures?

Ⓐ $2 \times \frac{3}{4}$ Ⓒ $6 \times \frac{1}{4}$

Ⓑ $6 \times \frac{1}{3}$ Ⓓ $8 \times \frac{1}{3}$

28 Bradley is training for a race. Today his coach wants him to run 3 miles. The running track is $\frac{1}{3}$ mile long. He has finished 5 laps. How many more miles does Bradley need to run?

Fill in the blanks with the correct answers from the list to complete and solve the equation.

$3 - ($ _____ $) = $ _____

4	5	$\frac{1}{3}$	$1\frac{1}{3}$
$3 \times \frac{1}{3}$		$5 \times \frac{1}{3}$	

29 Tamar catches a ball 12 times without dropping it. Malia catches a ball b times without dropping it. Malia catches 3 times as many times as Tamar.

Write an equation that shows how many times, b, Malia catches the ball without dropping it.

Equation: _____

$b = $ _____

30 The digits 0, 6, and 8 are used to make a three-digit number. The number is divided by 5.

Which of these numbers could be the remainder?

Select **all** the correct answers.

Ⓐ 0   Ⓓ 5

Ⓑ 2   Ⓔ 6

Ⓒ 3

---

31 Drew compares two fractions by comparing both fractions to $\frac{1}{2}$. He correctly reasons that fraction A is greater than fraction B because fraction A is greater than $\frac{1}{2}$ and fraction B is less than $\frac{1}{2}$.

Which of these could be the values of fractions A and B?

Ⓐ Fraction A is $\frac{2}{3}$ and fraction B is $\frac{3}{8}$.

Ⓑ Fraction A is $\frac{4}{10}$ and fraction B is $\frac{1}{4}$.

Ⓒ Fraction A is $\frac{5}{6}$ and fraction B is $\frac{10}{12}$.

Ⓓ Fraction A is $\frac{2}{5}$ and fraction B is $\frac{60}{100}$.

---

32 Which fraction is equivalent to 0.4?

Ⓐ $\frac{4}{10}$ Ⓒ $\frac{4}{100}$

Ⓑ $\frac{10}{4}$ Ⓓ $\frac{100}{4}$

33 The first number in a pattern is 6. The rule is "Multiply by 4."

Part A
What is the third number in the pattern?

Ⓐ 14   Ⓒ 96

Ⓑ 24   Ⓓ 384

Part B
Describe the features of the pattern.

Fill in the blanks with the correct words from the lists and circle the correct answers to complete the statements.

The numbers in the pattern _____ .

are all odd	are all even	alternate between even and odd

This is because ⏐ 4 / 6 ⏐ is ⏐ even / odd ⏐ and _____

_____ .

the product of a number and an odd number is even
the product of a number and an even number is odd
the product of a number and an even number is even

34 Shawn bakes 48 cookies for a school event. He shares 12 of them with his family. He places the remaining cookies equally into 9 snack bags.

- Write an equation that can be used to determine the number of cookies, c, that Shawn places into each snack bag.

- Find the number of cookies that Shawn places into each snack bag.

- Explain how you can check the reasonableness of your answer.

35 In an online learning game, students can earn badges for successfully completing a certain number of tasks based on what level of the game they are on. The number of tasks required to earn a badge at each level is shown in the table below.

Badge Requirements

Level	Number of Tasks
1	10
2	20
3	40
4	80
5	?

- If the pattern continues, write a number sentence that could be used to find the number of tasks the students will need to complete to earn a badge in level 5 of the game.

- Find the number of tasks that need to be completed to earn a badge in level 5.

- Based on the pattern, one student predicts that 240 tasks will need to be completed to earn a badge in level 6 of the game. Explain the error in the student's prediction. As part of your explanation, find the correct number of tasks that will need to be completed to earn a badge in level 6 of the game.

36 Marissa orders paper clips.

- She orders a case of paper clips. There are 6 different colors of paper clips in boxes of 54 paper clips. She gets 48 boxes in the case. What is the total number of paper clips in the case?

- The case has an equal number of each color of paper clips. One of the colors is blue. What is the total number of blue paper clips that she receives?

37 The table shows the sizes and amounts of soup in containers sold at a store.

Soup

Size	Amount of Soup (in cups)
Small	$\frac{3}{4}$
Medium	$\frac{5}{4}$
Large	$\frac{6}{4}$
Jumbo	$\frac{7}{4}$

- Maria bought 6 small containers of soup and Beau bought 5 large containers of soup. What is the difference in the amount of soup, in cups, of Maria's and Beau's purchases?

- Explain how you got your answer.

38 Matias is packing apples, oranges, granola bars, and water bottles for a hiking trip.

He packs 4 times as many water bottles as apples. He packs 2 times as many water bottles as granola bars. He packs 2 apples. How many granola bars and water bottles does Matias pack?

Matias packs 3 more oranges than apples. How many oranges does he pack?

Use equations or drawings to explain how you got your answer.

Name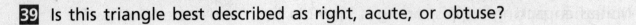

39 Is this triangle best described as right, acute, or obtuse?

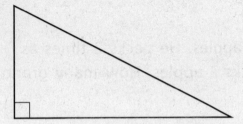

Explain how you know your answer is correct. Then explain why the other two choices are not correct.

1 Jonathan puts a fence around the perimeter of his rectangular lawn. The lawn measures 18 feet long by 12 feet wide.

How long in feet is the fence around his lawn?

(A) 30   (C) 108
(B) 60   (D) 216

---

2 Determine all the factors for the number 18.

Part A
Which list includes all of the factor pairs for 18?

(A) $2 \times 9, 3 \times 6, 18 \times 0$
(B) $1 \times 18, 2 \times 9, 3 \times 6$
(C) $1 \times 18, 2 \times 9, 3 \times 6, 4 \times 4$
(D) $0 \times 18, 2 \times 9, 3 \times 6, 4 \times 4$

Part B
Which of these numbers is a prime factor of 18?

Select **all** the answers that apply.

(A) 2   (D) 6
(B) 3   (E) 9
(C) 4   (F) 18

---

3 Paolo solves the equation $928 \div 4 = x$.

What is the value of x?

(A) 27   (C) 232
(B) 207   (D) 237

4 Miguel adds $\frac{2}{5} + \frac{2}{5}$ and gets the correct sum. What is another way that he can add fractions to get the same sum?

Ⓐ $\frac{2}{5} + \frac{1}{5} + \frac{1}{5}$

Ⓑ $\frac{1}{5} + \frac{2}{5} + \frac{2}{5}$

Ⓒ $\frac{2}{5} + \frac{3}{5} + \frac{1}{5}$

Ⓓ $\frac{1}{5} + \frac{1}{5} + \frac{1}{5} + \frac{1}{5} + \frac{1}{5}$

5 How many times greater is the 2 in the number 2,741 than the 2 in the number 283?

_____

6 Which comparison is true?

Ⓐ 0.24 > 0.28

Ⓑ 0.43 < 0.40

Ⓒ 0.67 < 0.68

Ⓓ 0.83 > 0.85

7 Angle G measures 90 degrees.

How many one-degree turns are there in angle G?

Ⓐ 30 Ⓒ 90

Ⓑ 60 Ⓓ 180

8 Kristen has to drive 808 miles in 5 days. She drives 180 miles the first day. Kristen plans to drive the same amount of miles each of the next 4 days.

If x represents the number of miles she drives each of those 4 days, what is the value of x?

x = _____

9 Which figure is an example of parallel lines?

Ⓐ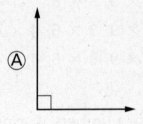

Ⓑ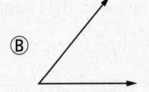

Ⓒ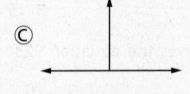

Ⓓ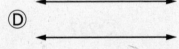

10 Which equations show a way to solve $312 \times 5 = x$?

Select **all** the correct answers.

Ⓐ $x = 300 \times 5 + 12$

Ⓑ $x = (300 + 5) \times 12$

Ⓒ $x = 300 + 10 + (2 \times 5)$

Ⓓ $x = (300 \times 5) + (12 \times 5)$

Ⓔ $x = (300 \times 5) + (10 \times 5) + (2 \times 5)$

---

11 What is the sum of $\frac{5}{10} + \frac{27}{100}$?

Ⓐ $\frac{77}{10}$

Ⓒ $\frac{77}{100}$

Ⓑ $\frac{32}{10}$

Ⓓ $\frac{32}{100}$

---

12 Lu took part in a 50-kilometer road race during the course of 3 days. Lu rode exactly $\frac{1}{2}$ the distance of the race on the first day. He rode $\frac{2}{5}$ of the remaining distance on the second day.

How many kilometers did he have left to ride on the last day?

---

13 Which of these is another way to write $\frac{2}{6} + \frac{4}{6} + \frac{1}{6}$?

Ⓐ $\frac{3}{6} + \frac{3}{6}$

Ⓒ $1 + \frac{1}{6}$

Ⓑ $\frac{7}{6} + \frac{1}{6}$

Ⓓ $\frac{1}{6} + \frac{2}{6} + \frac{4}{6} + 1$

14 Stefan is trying to determine which values properly balance the equations.

Part A

Which equations were solved correctly?

Select the **two** correct answers.

(A) $68 + 12 = n + 55$; $n = 5$

(B) $23 + 46 = s + 50$; $s = 9$

(C) $r + 20 = 14 + 43$; $r = 27$

(D) $70 + y = 68 + 14$; $y = 12$

(E) $20 + c = 5 + 31$; $c = 16$

Part B

Stefan looked at another equation on his list.

$20 + b = 22 + 7$; $b = 9$.

How could Stefan relate the left side of the equation to the right side of the equation to know that this equation was solved correctly?

(A) 22 minus 20 equals 2, and 9 minus 7 equals 2.

(B) 22 plus 7 is the same as 9 times 2 plus 2 plus 7.

(C) 22 plus 7 is 29, so the unknown must have a 9 in it.

(D) 20 is two less than 22, so the unknown must be 2 more than 7.

15 Maria is trying to determine an equivalent fraction to point *A* on the number line.

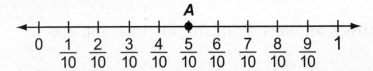

Which of these correctly explains the fraction that is equivalent to point *A* on the number line?

Ⓐ $\frac{4}{5}$ is equivalent because there are four positions before point *A*.

Ⓑ $\frac{1}{2}$ is equivalent because five parts out of ten is the same as one part out of two.

Ⓒ $\frac{2}{3}$ is equivalent because point *A* is two-thirds of the way to the end of the number line.

Ⓓ $\frac{1}{4}$ is equivalent because there are only four more fractions after point *A* until it reaches one whole.

---

16 Sal is trying to determine if these numbers are correctly rounded to the nearest hundred. Place an X in the table to show if the numbers are rounded correctly or incorrectly.

	Rounded Correctly	Rounded Incorrectly
1,275 rounded to 1,300		
2,752 rounded to 2,700		
3,629 rounded to 3,700		

17 Anna has 6 times as many marbles as Rachel. Rachel has 4 marbles. Create an equation to represent the situation.

Fill in the blanks with the correct answers from the list to complete the equation.

4 ___ ___ = ?

| + | ÷ | × | − | 4 | 6 |

---

18 Four angles are shown.

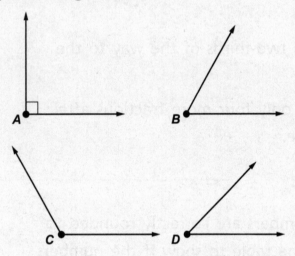

What are the measurements of these angles?

Draw a line from the angle to the correct angle measurement it matches.

Angle A	●	●	45°
Angle B	●	●	120°
Angle C	●	●	60°
Angle D	●	●	90°

19 A rectangle is 6 feet long and 3 feet wide. What are the length and width in inches of the rectangle?

Fill in the blanks with the correct answers from the list.

The rectangle is _____ inches long and _____ inches wide.

| 1 | 2 | 30 | 36 | 60 | 72 |

20 Which figure has a pair of perpendicular sides?

Ⓐ

Ⓑ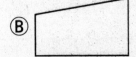

Ⓒ

Ⓓ

21 What is the value of n in the equation?

$$317 - n = 320 - 15$$

Ⓐ 5   Ⓒ 18

Ⓑ 12   Ⓓ 45

22 What is the measure of the unknown angle in the diagram?

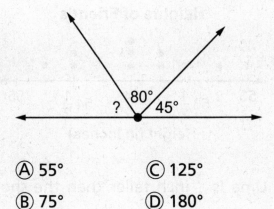

Ⓐ 55°   Ⓒ 125°

Ⓑ 75°   Ⓓ 180°

23 Lida draws a figure with exactly two lines of symmetry.

Which figures could Lida draw?

Select **all** the figures that Lida could draw.

Ⓐ

Ⓑ

Ⓒ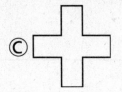

Ⓓ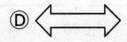

Ⓔ

24 Uma recorded the heights of 9 of her friends and displayed them in a line plot.

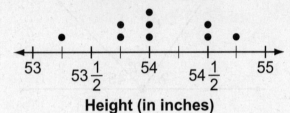

Heights of Friends

Height (in inches)

Uma is $\frac{3}{4}$ inch taller than the shortest friend. How tall is Uma?

Fill in the blanks with the correct answers from the list to complete the sentence.

The shortest height is _____ inches, so Uma is _____ inches tall.

| $52\frac{1}{2}$ | 53 | $53\frac{1}{4}$ | 54 | $54\frac{3}{4}$ | $55\frac{1}{2}$ |

25 Place an X in the table to tell whether each number is LESS than or GREATER than 305,268.

	Less than 305,268	Greater than 305,268
312,047		
$3 \times 10,000 + 5 \times 1,000 + 7 \times 100 + 1 \times 10 + 4$		
3 hundred thousands, 5 hundreds, 4 tens, 9 ones		

26 What is the sum of 23,614 and 158,630?

_____

27 Nathan makes a tower using blocks that are $\frac{5}{6}$ inch high. He stacks 14 blocks on top of each other.

How many inches tall is Nathan's tower?

Ⓐ $3\frac{1}{6}$ Ⓒ $14\frac{5}{6}$

Ⓑ $11\frac{4}{6}$ Ⓓ $16\frac{4}{5}$

28 Patrick wakes up at 7:15 a.m. He takes 30 minutes to get dressed and eat breakfast. He packs his lunch and then reads for 14 minutes before he leaves his house at 8:10 a.m.

How many minutes does Patrick take to pack his lunch?

Ⓐ 11   Ⓒ 21

Ⓑ 13   Ⓓ 26

29 At Evan's school, 26 students take French. If 3 times as many students take Spanish than French, how many students take Spanish at Evan's school?

_____

30 What is the quotient of 5,100 ÷ 6?

Ⓐ 850

Ⓑ 846 r4

Ⓒ 833 r2

Ⓓ 805

31 Which statement correctly compares $\frac{2}{5}$ and $\frac{3}{4}$?

Ⓐ $\frac{2}{5} < \frac{3}{4}$
because 3 is greater than 2.

Ⓑ $\frac{2}{5} > \frac{3}{4}$
because 5 is greater than 4.

Ⓒ $\frac{2}{5} < \frac{3}{4}$
because $\frac{3}{4}$ is greater than $\frac{1}{2}$ and $\frac{2}{5}$ is less than $\frac{1}{2}$.

Ⓓ $\frac{2}{5} > \frac{3}{4}$
because $\frac{2}{5}$ is greater than $\frac{1}{2}$ and $\frac{3}{4}$ is less than $\frac{1}{2}$.

32 Plot a point on the number line that is equal to $\frac{6}{10}$.

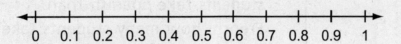

---

33 The first number in a pattern is 40. The pattern follows the rule "Subtract 6." What are the next 3 numbers in the pattern?

Numbers in the Pattern
40

34 Gemma picks 80 peaches from a peach tree. She uses 17 of them to make peach cobbler. She places the remaining peaches equally into 9 gift baskets.

- Write an equation that can be used to determine the number of peaches, p, that Gemma places into each gift basket.

- Find the number of peaches Gemma places into each gift basket.

- Explain how you can check the reasonableness of your answer.

Name

35 Mrs. Dawson reads the same number of books to her class each week. The table below shows the total number of books that Mrs. Dawson has read to her class at the end of weeks 2, 3, and 4.

Mrs. Dawson's Books

Week	Number of Books
2	8
3	12
4	16
5	?

- If the pattern continues, write a number sentence that could be used to find the total number of books that Mrs. Dawson will read to her students at the end of week 5.

- Find the total number of books that Mrs. Dawson reads to her students at the end of week 5.

- Based on the pattern, one of the students in Mrs. Dawson's class makes the statement that Mrs. Dawson will read a total of 80 books over the course of a 9-week marking period. Explain the error in the student's statement. As part of your explanation, find the correct number of books that Mrs. Dawson will read over the course of a 9-week marking period.

36 A nursery owner grows 8 different types of bushes.

- She grows the bushes on her 56-acre farm. She grows 32 bushes per acre. What is the total number of bushes growing on her farm?

- The nursery owner grows an equal number of each type of bush. One of the types of bush that she grows is lilac. What is the total number of lilac bushes that she grows?

37 The table shows the sizes and weights of bags of mixed nuts sold at a store.

Mixed Nuts

Size	Weight (in pounds)
Small	$\frac{1}{8}$
Medium	$\frac{3}{8}$
Large	$\frac{7}{8}$
Jumbo	$\frac{11}{8}$

- Steve buys 9 medium bags of mixed nuts and Alice buys 3 jumbo bags of mixed nuts. What is the difference in the weights, in pounds, of Steve's and Alice's purchases?

- Explain how you got your answer.

38 Alp's dog has a lot of toys.

He has tennis balls, chewing toys, and squeaking toys. He has 4 times as many tennis balls as squeaking toys. He has 2 times as many tennis balls as chewing toys. He has 4 squeaking toys. How many tennis balls and chewing toys does Alp's dog have?

Alp has two fewer leashes for his dog than the number of squeaking toys. How many leashes does he have?

Use equations or drawings to explain how you got your answer.

39 Is this triangle best described as right, acute, or obtuse?

Explain how you know your answer is correct. Then explain why the other two choices are not correct.